Vegan Cookbook

Tasty Recipes and Tips for Your Health

WHITE STAR PUBLISHERS

Photographs and Recipes
CINZIA TRENCHI

Project Editor
VALERIA MANFERTO DE FABIANIS

Graphic Design
MARIA CUCCHI

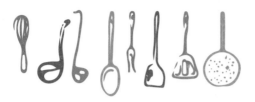

INTRODUCTION

The Properties of Basic Foods and How to Use Them

Recipes

Introduction

It is now widely
known that a diet based
on legumes, grains, vegetables and
fruit is a passport to well-being and life
energy. Considering the limited impact that
a diet of this type has on the environment,
it is almost an inevitable choice. Philosophy,
or healthy benefits? Veganism is both; provided that one
is aware of both the benefits and difficulties involved.
Besides being a source of nourishment, food, as we
know, is also about conviviality; it plays a fundamental
part in our celebrations, our friendships, doing business.
Veganism involves making sacrifices which may seem
insurmountable, especially until you know which foods can
be used to substitute steaks, poultry, eggs, fish, sugar, honey,
and so on.
This book isn't meant to be a philosophical work on the eth-
ics of your diet: it is intended to be a tool for learning more
about what are essentially new dietary rules (veganism was born
in England in 1944), and discovering how, thanks to the abundance
of legumes, the versatility of grains and the adaptability of dried

fruits, seasonal vegetables, seeds, spices and herbs, you can go from an omnivorous diet to one that is a free of protein, animal fats and animal-based derivatives. Often the difficulties found in using new flavors and bizarre, almost unthinkable combinations, are due to lack of experience. This book contains easy recipes, many of which are quick, and useful tips on how to get around the amount of time spent on preparing and cooking food; time that most of us don't have.

Four sections to explore and experiment with the value of foods; starting with grains, flours and cream soups; moving on to legumes, found in seeds or in the form of "cheeses" and drinks; then vegetables, an inexhaustible source of fiber, carbohydrates and vitamins; and finally fruit, which when fresh are a vital source of hydration, and when dry they integrate sugars and minerals, important for our well-being, into our diet.

Vegan is designed to offer practical help to all those who wish to make this important choice, and who need help in the kitchen to turn dishes into appetizing, tasty recipes that make your mouth water just thinking about them. It contains valuable tips for a diet that replaces the pillars of omnivorous cuisine and introduc- es what are often little-known foods into everyday cooking. But the real question is how do you make "mayonnaise"? Sauces are fundamental, and with oat cream, corn oil and mustard, or blended avocado and spices, you can create tasty accompaniments for your steamed vegetables. And to make grains and flours look yummy? In addition to colorful seasonal vegetables, another important resource is seeds, small gems that are full of flavor and with properties that are beneficial to our well-being. Linseeds, poppy, sesame or pumpkin seeds; great to look at, adding color to your dishes, and, thanks to the different textures, putting crunchiness in every bite. Aromatic herbs are also a key ingredient, perfecting dishes with their aroma and adding a decorative touch. How a dish looks is most definitely an important part of cooking, however simple it is, and it should be presented in the best possible way, so that changing your diet is not a sacrifice, but something that enriches your life.

Condiments also play a vital role. We can substitute butter with vegetable butter, very useful for both sweet and savory preparations; or we can mix hazelnut, walnut and peanut oils, either together or with extra virgin olive oil: besides being beauty's best friends, they are wonderful for dressing salads, soups and cakes. The sourness of umeboshi vinegar, apple vinegar, lemon and orange juice can also be used to add a touch of flavor to salads, making them even more delicious. And while we're on the subject of dressings, what has the soybean got to offer? Whether it is in the form of "butter" or "milk", oil, agglomerates, cream, tofu or other derivatives, the soybean is such a versatile and tasty food that it is impossible to ignore: in whatever form, it can be used in liberally! Furthermore, it can help solve many small problems in the kitchen.

However, let's not forget that any food in our diet must be one of many; not the only one. This applies above all to processed and alterable foods: we can integrate them into our diet, but in moderation, and this not only applies to the soybean, but also to rice, wheat and corn!

Turmeric, any variety of chili pepper — however hot — curry powder, pepper, seasonings of different varieties and colors: use them without fear of being overwhelmed by strong flavors. Experts highlight how beneficial they are for our well-being thanks to the presence of valuable substances for our body. Let's also not forget the role of salt, which must be coarse and used sparingly. Choose it for its color or texture and only add it after cooking, that way you use less and appreciate the taste of the dish more. And instead of milk? Equally nutritious and tasty beverages, based on oats, rice, soybeans, almonds and coconut; you can make them at home or buy them ready-made; they are perfect for sauces, desserts, ice creams or as a refreshing mineral rich drink. And what about sugar and honey? Sweeteners are viewed with certain indifference in a vegan diet. For those who just can't give them up, acceptable alternatives include brown sugar or, even better, malt, although the best choice remains the natural sugar found in fruits. Date puree is an excellent alternative for sweetening desserts, as are figs, almonds, the pulp of ripe banana and coconut flour.

With a variety of textures, ingredients and new combinations to choose from, there are infinite ways to indulge yourself, aware that you are doing something "good" not only for your own well-being, but also for that of our planet.

Vegan Tidbits

The first step is to slowly eliminate foods of animal origin and to gradually integrate those which are not part of our family's diet history. Experts are increasingly in agreement about recommending low or protein-free diets, including animal-derived substances. In addition to the considerable cost in terms of environmental impact, basing a diet on foods of animal origin appears to be one of the main causes of serious health problems. We should diversify our diet, try to eat different foods every day, so that our body can absorb those elements that are beneficial to our well-being; seasonal fruit and vegetables should always be present. Food and life; an "inseparable duo" that we must never lose sight of. All food is precious. Its energy content shouldn't be messed with and, above all, its true nature must be respected: for example, in winter don't eat foods that ripen in the summer. Prepare simple but colorful dishes; dishes that smell good and look great. It may seem trivial, but it definitely helps to mitigate the feeling of sacrifice that comes with a diet. Approach a diet as important as a vegan one with respect for the limitations that it imposes; consult a specialist if you feel debilitated. Any food choice we make should improve our vitality; make us feel stronger, fitter and happy. Where possible, try to choose foods whose origin you can be certain of; locally produced foods that are preferably fresh, seasonal and organic. Eat when you're hungry; we shouldn't force ourselves to include or eliminate foods, dressings or flavors.

The right diet is
not one based on
sacrifice; unless you have
to follow specific
guidelines due to health
problems.
Good eating
habits include
seasonal fresh fruit
and vegetables, which,
to keep your body
healthy, should be
supplemented with
carbohydrates, proteins
and vegetable fats.
In any diet, and especially in a vegan diet,
the digestive system must be protected and
nourished: eat foods that are rich in prebiotics
(fibers) that will nourish the probiotics (such as
those contained in miso and fermented vegetables),
thereby ensuring healthy intestinal flora.

OATS

We can find oats in the form of groats, flakes, flour, cream and beverages. It is extremely rich in protein, high in fiber and helps keep cholesterol low. The seed remains intact during processing, without altering the lipid content. Iron, calcium, potassium, phosphorus and zinc are minerals that make this carbohydrate a pillar of a vegan diet. Sweet and pleasant-tasting, oat is suitable for making cookies, cakes, bars, sweet and savory soups. Oat cream is excellent for using in pasta dishes, risottos and vegetable parcels.

Annual herbaceous plant whose seed is gluten-free and therefore recommended for those with celiac disease. Easy to digest, it has a high percentage of protein, dietary fiber, sugars, vitamin A and minerals such as iron, calcium, potassium, magnesium and zinc. It helps strengthen the hair and nails thanks to the presence of silicic acid; a true ally in beauty and our well-being. It comes in the form of flour, groats and flakes, and is perfect for making soups, millet balls, cakes and cookies, either together with other grains or on its own. As it is gluten-free, it tends not to stick together very well when making cakes and bread.

BULGUR

Cracked wheat is a very ancient food and you can buy it both raw and cooked. In the latter case, the groats are steamed and then diced. Either way, it's not hard to prepare it from the seeds at home. Bulgur has the same properties as wholegrain wheat: it is high in carbohydrates, has a good percentage of protein (about 13%) and contains fiber that is beneficial to the digestive process. It is rich in iron, zinc, calcium, potassium and phosphorus. This grain contains large quantities of Niacin, also known as vitamin B3 or PP, which contributes to protecting mucous, and folic acid, otherwise known as vitamin B9.

One of the first products cultivated by
man, wheat is divided into durum wheat
(richer in gluten and protein) and soft
wheat (hardly any fibers). High-energy
and the base of the Mediterranean
diet, it is a great source of iron,
calcium, potassium, phosphorus, zinc,
thiamine and folic acid. Combined
with legumes it can be a substitute
for protein and animal derivatives.
It is best to alternate the use of
wheat in flour, pasta or bread with
the groats, which retain all of the
beneficial properties.

WHEAT

MILLET

SEITAN

This is dough made from gluten
(mainly wheat), cooked and
enriched with Kombu seaweed
and soy sauce. In the shops you
can find it in its natural form,
grilled, cubed or sliced. But how
can you make it at home? Just add
water to the flour and mix with
your hands to separate the proteins
(which tend to agglomerate) from the
other components. Seitan is an excellent
ingredient for dishes with a firm texture,
as it is like meat and has important nutritional
properties.

BUCKWHEAT

Triangular buckwheat groats are very rich in starch and protein. They contain lysine and tryptophan, essential amino acids for our diet. It appears that it is able to keep blood sugar levels low and "bad" cholesterol at bay. It is gluten-free and therefore recommended for those with celiac disease. It should be eaten regularly in the form of groats or flour (for example, for making pizzoccheri pasta); the groats are perfect for adding to soups or salads, and the flour for making crepes and breads. It has a fresh and pleasant taste.

WHOLEMEAL FLOUR

BARLEY

Barley is a cereal grain belonging to the grass family, not recommended for those with celiac disease. Low in fat and easy to digest, there are 319 calories per 100 grams (3.5 oz.), with 10% protein. Rich in potassium, magnesium, iron, silicon and zinc, it is an important source of minerals and due to the vitamins present, E and B-group, it is a fundamental ingredient in a vegan diet. If you have celiac disease, it is important to remember that malt, beer and whiskey are barley-based products.

The common name for *Chenopodium quinoa*, The small seeds of this cereal grain are an important component in diets with a reduced intake of animal protein. Quinoa is rich in vitamin E, iron, and vitamin C. For those with celiac disease it is an excellent alternative to classic grains containing gluten. It is easy to prepare (it cooks in about 20 minutes). The flour mixes well with wheat flour, and the groats are ideal for making soups, quinoa balls and salads.

QUINOA

As it is richer in nutrients, wholemeal flour should be used in any diet. It is important in a vegan diet because it maintains the original levels of mineral salts, vitamins, fiber, protein, carbohydrates, etc. of the plant. Ideally the groats should be ground at the time of eating, so as to maintain all the components intact and active: there are a wide range of appliances available on the market for grinding the grains into flour, but only in small quantities and therefore only suitable for home cooking.

WHOLEGRAIN PASTA

It goes without saying that wholegrain pasta is a balanced food and recommended in a vegan diet due to its beneficial properties. It alters depending on the flour used to make it (wheat, spelt, buckwheat etc.), but wholegrain pasta definitely maintains the fiber, vitamins and minerals of the original cereal grain.

WHITE RICE

Easily digestible and assimilated, white rice is recommended for those with digestive problems. It is a gluten-free cereal grain, suitable for those with celiac disease. Although rich in calcium, potassium and phosphorus, it is low in fiber and vitamins like niacin and folic acid. It is great for preparing many tasty dishes, but can also be used to make "milk" and condiments such as oil, with which you can add finishing touches to delicious and flavorsome dishes.

Venus rice, or black rice, is naturally colored and fragrant; it is perfect when boiled in a little water and then sautéed with vegetables, oil-rich seeds, fresh herbs and spices. It contains anthocyanins, which are really good for protecting cells against free radicals. It is a source of iron and selenium (it is a regulator of intestinal function), it lowers "bad" cholesterol and increases "good" cholesterol. Easily digestible, it is recommended in the diets of children and the elderly.

BROWN RICE

In contrast to white rice, brown rice is rich in fiber and highly recommended for those who suffer from a sluggish bowel. With a high vitamin and mineral content, brown rice is particularly suitable for those wishing to follow a diet without proteins and animal derivatives. It can be used in any kind of dish and maintains a nice texture when used for making risotto, but it is also delicious in dishes that have a longer-cooking time, like minestrones and soups, making them really creamy.

A naturally red, wholegrain rice with a fresh, distinctive taste. Although it needs to cook for a fairly long time (about 40 minutes), it maintains a unique texture that makes it perfect for salads or mixing with fruit and vegetables. It is ideal in diets as it has a high Satiety Index. It's also indicated for high cholesterol as it contributes to regulating values, lowering those which are harmful (LDL) and increasing those which are beneficial (HDL). It is a valuable source of vitamin B6, iron, manganese and zinc.

RED RICE

VENUS RICE

WILD RICE

Wild rice (*Zizania aquatica*) is a spontaneous grass that is assimilated to rice due to its organoleptic characteristics. It has long thin grains that vary in color, ranging from dark brown to dark red and brown. It needs to cook for a long time and has a distinctive flavor that makes it perfect for serving with boring vegetables. Naturally wholegrain, it is rich in calcium, magnesium, potassium, phosphorus and zinc.

WHITE CHICKPEAS

Seeds from the annual herbaceous plant *Cicer arietinum*, of the legume family. Chickpeas are rich in proteins, starches, fats, B-group vitamins and vitamin E. They contain calcium, potassium, phosphorus and zinc. They are perfect for creating delicious dishes such as salads, cream soups, soups and focaccia bread. It is worth knowing that the stock obtained from boiling them, sipped several times during the day, promotes diuresis.

KIDNEY BEANS

Soft, sweet and reminiscent of the flavor and texture of chestnuts. Like other beans, they are a great meat substitute, especially when combined with other foods such as carbohydrates, fruit and vegetables. It's absolutely true that beans favor the formation of intestinal gas: to avoid embarrassing situations, when cooking simply add a teaspoon of grated ginger, or a piece of Kombu seaweed, or herbs and spices like savory, cumin, coriander and garlic.

BLACK CHICKPEAS

Black chickpeas differ from white ones due to the intense color of the skin, which makes them extremely pleasing to the eye. As with all dried legumes, they need to be soaked before using. There are 334 calories per 100 grams (3.5 oz.). They are a great help in lowering LDL cholesterol, thereby helping to improve blood circulation. Thanks to the presence of fiber and complex carbohydrates, they leave you with a pleasant feeling of satiety.

Beans are one of the pillars of a vegetarian and vegan diet, and the nutritional components of the various different varieties are very similar. They are universally considered as the "poor man's meat" given the presence of proteins and complex carbohydrates. They integrate perfectly with other carbohydrates. Borlotti beans are highly prized for their flavor and texture: depending on how they're cooked, they can be used to make a smooth and creamy soup.

BORLOTTI BEANS

These small red beans are great for our well-being. Also known as red soybeans, they are a popular ingredient in Japan and used for many delicious dishes. Rich in minerals such as potassium and zinc, and high in fiber, Azuki beans have depurative properties, contribute to strengthening the immune system and are particularly indicated in vegan diets. Ideal in soups and salads, there are 270 calories per 100 grams (3.5 oz.).

AZUKI

BLACK BADDA BEANS

Beautiful black and white beans that resemble the yin and yang sign, grown in the Madonie National Park in Sicily. They have a very savory flavor and when cooked they become creamy without flaking apart. They are easily digestible and ideal in soups and salads. Like other bean varieties, they are rich in B-group vitamins and vitamins A and C, fiber and minerals such as iron, magnesium and potassium. There are about 100 calories per 100 grams (3.5 oz.) of fresh product.

CHICKLING PEAS

Chickling peas, whose scientific name is *Lathyrus sativus*, belong to the legume family. The seeds are very rich in protein, high-energy, easily digestible and apparently indicated for lowering high cholesterol. They need to be soaked for a very long time before using, even one or two days, and the water should be changed several times. This procedure reduces or removes the toxic properties of the seeds, which if eaten frequently and in abundance can cause the lathyrism syndrome.

Seeds of the herbaceous plant *Lens culinaris*, belonging to the legume family. Lentils are rich in proteins and very easy to digest. They contain very little water and fats and are high in dietary fiber, which stimulates bowel movements. Its valuable components are also able to regulate cholesterol levels. It has a high calorific value: 325 calories per 100 grams (3.5 oz.). Lentils can be cooked in minestrone and soups, served in salads, and, in the form of flour, used for making sauces, condiments and desserts.

GIGANTE BEANS

Although they all belong to the legume family, beans vary in size (from small to large) and color (bright colors to delicate hues). Gigante beans, like Runner or Lima beans, are great to look at and ideal in salads. They should be soaked for a few hours (about 8-10) to make the skin softer and more elastic, and to prevent splitting during cooking. They are a valuable source of protein in a vegan diet. They have a high Satiety Index and are highly nutritious: 330 calories per 100 grams (3.5 oz.) of dried beans.

Annual herbaceous plant that produces seed pods, belonging to the legume family. Fava beans can be eaten fresh in spring, even raw, or dried, prior to soaking and cooking. They are high in proteins, carbohydrates, fats and minerals such as potassium, phosphorus and calcium, and vitamins like C, folic acid and retinol. They are a very important food for vegans because of the high protein content. 37 calories per 100 grams (3.5 oz.) of fresh beans and around 300 calories for dried beans.

FAVA BEANS

LENTILS

WILD PEAS

These small brown seeds were commonly harvested and dried for the preparation of traditional "poor man's" dishes. Once considered a weed, they have gradually disappeared from flower beds and lawns, but thanks to their fans they are not entirely extinct. With a pea pod similar to common peas, they contain a wealth of beneficial nutrients to include in your diet and make you feel good: in fact, they contain minerals such as potassium, phosphorus, and vitamins like B1. They taste great, and the dried seeds can be ground into flour and transformed into an amazing polenta!

TOFU

Tofu is the Japanese name for soybean cheese. It is obtained from curdling soy milk (liquid produced by leaving soybeans to soak in water for about 24 hours). It is a neutral tasting food that has the amazing ability of absorbing any seasoning or flavor that is added to it. Low in calories and extremely satiating, tofu is rich in antioxidants and is a key ally in keeping cholesterol at optimum levels.

GREEN SOYBEANS

SOYA BUTTER

This is an all-natural alternative for preparing all those cookies, puff pastries and dishes that require the use of butter. With a little patience you can make it yourself. By mixing soy milk with oil, lecithin and apple cider vinegar you will get a 100% vegetable butter. Great flavor and texture, there are 630 calories per 100 grams (3.5 oz.).

Soya chunks are pieces of textured soy flour. Once cooked, their consistency is very much like that of meat and thanks to their properties they are in fact a substitute for animal proteins. The chunks are available in different sizes and are ideal for making ragu or stews, as well as a wide range of other yummy high protein dishes. The pieces of textured soy flour maintain the basic characteristics of the legume and are therefore an excellent food in a vegan diet.

SOY NUGGETS

Soybeans are one of the most digestible legumes and are suitable for vegan diets thanks to their high protein content. Green soybeans are about 70% water and contain minerals such as potassium, phosphorus, calcium, zinc, iron, and vitamins A, B1, B2, B3, B5, B6 and C. The presence of lecithin is important, as it is able to emulsify fats. It also appears that soybeans are able to counteract hormone-sensitive tumors.

SMOKED TOFU

In a vegan diet one must accept that food is generally less appetizing, and despite being a healthy food, tofu is by no stretch of the imagination "good" if not accompanied by spices, herbs and seasonings. Thanks to smoked tofu, it is possible to cook dishes with the same nutritional value but with a much stronger flavor. You can therefore make sauces for adding flavor to rice, pasta or boiled vegetables, making the dish much more appetizing.

GARLIC

Garlic is a herbaceous plant belonging to the lily family, well-known for its power to flavor foods and its active ingredients, which are encased in a bulb... with therapeutic properties! Its cloves are able to balance the intestinal flora and help reduce the oxidation of fats, by preventing the formation of free radicals. They act on "bad" cholesterol, promote diuresis and contribute to lowering high blood pressure.

CHINESE CABBAGE

SEAWEED

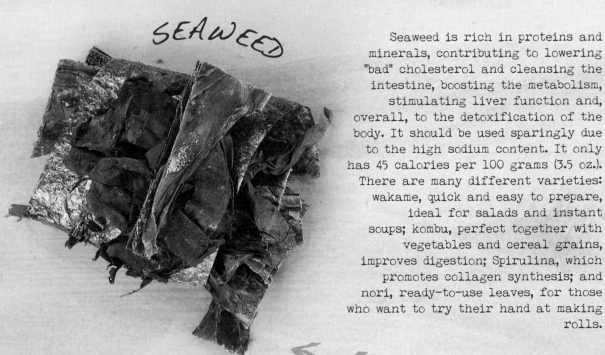

Seaweed is rich in proteins and minerals, contributing to lowering "bad" cholesterol and cleansing the intestine, boosting the metabolism, stimulating liver function and, overall, to the detoxification of the body. It should be used sparingly due to the high sodium content. It only has 45 calories per 100 grams (3.5 oz.). There are many different varieties: wakame, quick and easy to prepare, ideal for salads and instant soups; kombu, perfect together with vegetables and cereal grains, improves digestion; Spirulina, which promotes collagen synthesis; and nori, ready-to-use leaves, for those who want to try their hand at making rolls.

Brussels sprouts are actually the buds that grow on the stem of the plant. They contain isothiocyanate and indole compounds, which are able to offer protection against cancer. Excellent for preparing smoothies and fresh juices, Brussel sprouts are great for mineralizing and detoxifying the body. They have a high water content, calcium, potassium, phosphorus and vitamins such as C, folic acid and retinol. Low in calories (only 37 calories per 100 grams / 3.5 oz.), like broccoli and cabbage it is generally better to eat them in the fall and winter, when "in season".

BRUSSELS SPROUTS

It belongs to the cruciferous family and is rich in thiocyanate, believed to possess anti-cancer properties. Chinese cabbage contributes to lowering "bad" cholesterol and, thanks to its extremely low calorific value (about 14 calories per 100 grams / 3.5 oz.!), it is highly recommended in diets to lose weight. With its delicate flavor, it is good raw, using just the green leaves, blanched or stir-fried, including the white part. It has a very high water and vitamin A content.

Potassium, calcium, phosphorus and large quantities of folic acid: broccoli is a treasure trove of fiber and nutrients. Rich in vitamin C, it is one of the best fall vegetables to combat the cold and seasonal ailments. It is an antioxidant and has an excellent cleansing effect due to its diuretic properties; it is said to have anti-tumor properties and helps combat macular degeneration. It's perfect for slimming diets: it contains only 27 calories per 100 grams (3.5 oz.) and over 90% water. It is delicious raw in crudités, lightly cooked and in soups and minestrones.

BROCCOLI

CABBAGE

It is 92% water, low in calories (just 19 calories per 100 grams / 3.5 oz.), and an essential food, especially in the cold months, because of the high vitamin C content. It has always been considered to have medicinal properties, improving the well-being and health of both adults and children. It helps cleanse the body: thanks to its compounds and fibers it regulates bowel movements, detoxifies the liver and improves overall physical appearance.

EGGPLANT

RADICCHIO

A vegetable of various shapes, sizes and colors, radicchio (Cichorium intybus) belongs to the Composite or Asteraceae family, and, like common chicory, derives from wild chicory. It only contains 13 calories per 100 grams (3.5 oz.) and is 94% water; thanks to its fibers it helps regulate bowel movements. It contains folic acid, vitamin C, calcium, potassium and phosphorus. It is great raw in salads or slightly blanched. For a decoction with digestive and diuretic effects, boil 2-3 leaves in 1 dl (3.4 fl. oz.) of water.

The carrot is the root of the herbaceous plant *Daucus carota*. It can be found year-round in various colors, ranging from white to dark purple. The nutritional properties of this vegetable make it a great ally in our well-being: it protects the gastric and intestinal mucosa, stimulates diuresis and helps regulate bowel movements. It is rich in beta-carotene, which the body metabolizes in the form of vitamin A. Revitalizing and anti-inflammatory, it is excellent raw, as a snack to put hunger at bay, or in soups, stews, fresh juices and smoothies.

CARROT

It is the fruit of the annual plant *Solanum melongena*. There are various types, with different shapes and colors: the most common are purple and can be oval, round or long. The skin contains dietary fiber, minerals such as calcium, phosphorus and potassium, B-group vitamins and vitamin C, so it is best not to remove it. This vegetable is low in calories and can promote diuresis and improve liver function.

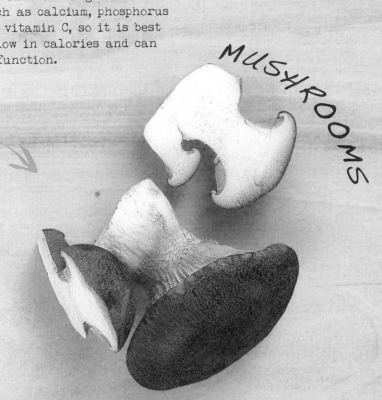

MUSHROOMS

You can find different types of mushrooms depending on the season. In particular, the "cardoncelli" variety grows in spring and summer: they are low in calories (28 calories per 100 grams / 3.5 oz.), contain all of the essential amino acids and have a high water and protein content. They are highly recommended in a vegan diet. They also contain iron, calcium, potassium and phosphorus. In general mushrooms are very delicate and must be consumed soon after purchase.

Whether it is hot, really hot or mild enough for all palates, chili peppers as well as being a valuable ally in our well-being, is able to transform a dish into an unforgettable sensory experience! Rich in retinol and vitamin C, its spicy personality tantalizes the taste buds and digestive processes. There are many varieties and can be found either fresh or dried; as well as making any dish decidedly more exiting, it is also used to make mind-blowing chili sauce.

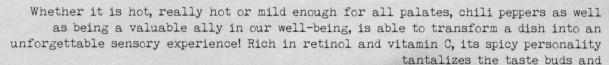

CHILI PEPPER

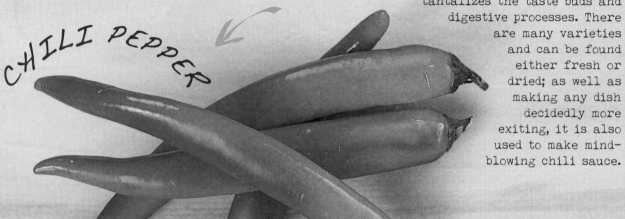

OLIVES

The pepper plant is annual and belongs to the Solanaceae family. Its fresh tasting fruit, with fleshy, crunchy pulp, is rich in vitamin C and retinol. Low in calories (22 calories per 100 grams / 3.5 oz.),

pepper has a high water content and is highly recommended in diets to lose weight. It gives a distinct flavor to dishes and the bright colors create appetizing and irresistible appetizers, main courses and side dishes.

PEPPER

Related to garlic and onion, the
leek belongs to the lily family and
ripens between summer and winter.
It is low in fat, proteins and
sugar, yet rich in vitamins (niacin,
folic acid, C) and minerals (calcium,
sodium, potassium and phosphorus).
It has very few calories: 27 per 100
grams (3.5 oz.). It has a high water
content, promoting diuresis and
regular bowel movements. With its
wonderful flavor and texture, it
is an exceptional ingredient for
soups and vegetable stews.

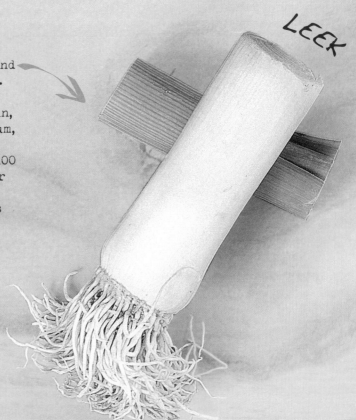

LEEK

They are the fruits of the *Olea europaea* plant, belonging to the Oleaceae family.
Typical of the Mediterranean basin since time immemorial, they are a food that
stimulates the appetite, at the same time promoting digestion and regular bowel
movements. They promote an increase in "good" cholesterol and are extremely high-
calorie and high-energy. They contain important elements with antioxidant properties
and vitamins such as C and folic acid. You can find them in brine, dried, pickled or
seasoned.

In nature,
the *Solanum
lycopersicum*
plant produces fruits in myriad
colors, shapes (round or oblong) and
sizes (as small as a cherry or up to
1 kg / 2 lb. in weight). A tomato is 94%
water and, with just 17 calories per 100
grams (3.5 oz.), is a valuable a food in low-
calorie diets. Rich in lycopene, it helps lower
"bad" cholesterol, triglycerides and free radicals.
Best eaten fresh, especially in summer, the tomato is ideal in
salads and refreshing juices.

TOMATO

SCALLION

Related to garlic and onions, it tastes similar to both, although not as strong. It is greater than 92% water, with 20 calories per 100 grams (3.5 oz.). It is a valuable ingredient for flavoring dishes and stocking up on substances that are beneficial to our well-being. It contains retinol (vitamin A) in large quantities, vitamin C, folic acid and minerals such as potassium, phosphorus, calcium, zinc and sulfur. Due to the selenium present in the bulb, it is an anti-aging food.

PUMPKIN

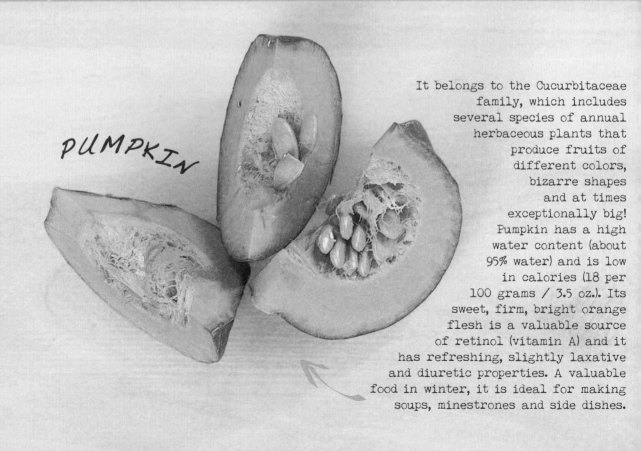

It belongs to the Cucurbitaceae family, which includes several species of annual herbaceous plants that produce fruits of different colors, bizarre shapes and at times exceptionally big! Pumpkin has a high water content (about 95% water) and is low in calories (18 per 100 grams / 3.5 oz.). Its sweet, firm, bright orange flesh is a valuable source of retinol (vitamin A) and it has refreshing, slightly laxative and diuretic properties. A valuable food in winter, it is ideal for making soups, minestrones and side dishes.

POTATO

Like tomatoes, peppers and eggplants, potatoes, tuber of the herbaceous plant *Solanum tuberosum*, belong to the Solanaceae family. There are many varieties: white, yellow, purple, sweet. A staple food for many populations in the world, they are nutritious and easy to digest. Their high starch content makes them a great substitute for pasta and bread, but with less calories (about 70 calories per 100 grams / 3.5 oz. when boiled). They are rich in potassium, phosphorus, and vitamins such as C and folic acid.

ZUCCHINI

A zucchini is the immature fruit of the annual plant *Cucurbita pepo*. The peel has various color gradations, varying from light yellow to deep green. It is a summer vegetable and an excellent ingredient for salads, either raw or cooked. Versatile and filling, it is a valuable food for those with digestive problems. It has a very high water content (about 95% of their weight), with 100 calories per 100 grams (3.5 oz.). It contains minerals such as calcium, iron, potassium and phosphorus, and vitamins E, C and beta-carotene.

ORANGE

The orange is a winter fruit that are rich in vitamin C, folic acid and retinol. Its thirst-quenching juice is a vitamin-booster and has toning properties. It is recommended in fighting colds, combatting free radicals and, thanks to the calcium and potassium, promoting cellular activity. Low in calories (just 34 calories per 100 grams / 3.5 oz.), it contains fiber that help regulate bowel movements. Excellent when eaten sliced and freshly squeezed, it is also ideal for creating fresh and tasty salads.

LEMON

Fruit and condiment, the lemon is a treasure trove of beneficial properties for our well-being: anti-inflammatory, antiseptic, cleansing the intestines and liver. Thirst-quenching when freshly squeezed, it can help with indigestion: the ascorbic acid makes it a completely natural gastric antacid. Furthermore, in winter it helps to fight colds. Thanks to the considerable amount of vitamin C, it contributes to the formation of collagen fibers, hydrates the skin and restores brightness.

Fruit of the *Citrus nobilis*, it is rich in sugar, about 72 calories per 100 grams (3.5 oz.), very refreshing and, thanks to the sweet and satisfying taste, ideal for squeezing into cooked and raw dishes to sweeten them naturally. Rich in vitamins such as C, retinol and folic acid, this winter fruit should not be overlooked. Moreover, thanks to its dietary fiber, it stimulates intestinal activity.

MANDARIN

KUMQUAT

The kumquat, of the *Fortunella* genus, is a small citrus fruit that are easy to grow in the garden or in pots on a balcony; in winter the fruit appears in abundance on the minute and pretty plants. It has an intense flavor and aroma, with a sweet peel but very tangy juice. Very refreshing, it can be eaten whole, either cooked or raw. Rich in vitamin A and C, it is also a good source of calcium. It has about 70 calories per 100 grams (3.5 oz.).

APRICOT

It is easily digestible and rich in carotenoids. 100 grams (3.5 oz.) of ripe apricots provide almost half of the daily vitamin A intake necessary for an adult. It also contains vitamins B1, B2, C and PP, as well as minerals such as potassium, calcium, phosphorus and magnesium. It is high-energy and can increase the body's natural defenses. Low in calories and with a high water content, it is an ideal, satisfying snack, either as it is or in juices and smoothies. Due to its slightly laxative action it is indicated for a lazy bowel, especially in its dried form.

BANANA

Sweet, high-energy, nutritious; it is one of the most consumed fruits in the world, not only because it's tasty, but also because, thanks to its nutrients, it is recommended for adults and children. Available year-round, its dietary fiber helps regulate bowel movements. It contains potassium, iron, magnesium, phosphorus, vitamin A and C, simple and complex sugars, and a little water. It has 66 calories per 100 grams (3.5 oz.) and is recommended for all those who engage in sports and intellectual activities.

MELON

Fruit of the *Cucumis melo*, it is 90% water and low calorie (33 calories per 100 grams / 3.5 oz.): not only is it fresh and refreshing, but also cleansing, diuretic and able to help regulate bowel movements. It is a true ally in low-calorie diets, as well as in contrasting emotional eating. A typically summer food, it helps to combat the heat and, like all orange fruits, thanks to its vitamins, it promotes tanning. It is excellent eaten sliced, when fully ripe, and its compactness makes it an ideal ingredient for fruit salads, smoothies and beverages.

BLUEBERRIES

Small berries with an intense blue-black color, fruit of the shrub *Vaccinium myrtillus*, they ripen in summer but can be found in supermarkets almost all year. Beneficial to the sight and capillaries, they also have digestive and antiseptic properties, contain vitamin A and C, iron, manganese, potassium, phosphorus, and even tannins and anthocyanins, which experts indicate as allies against aging. Low in calories (when fresh about 30 calories per 100 grams /3.5 oz.), they are ideal for making smoothies, sauces, jams and desserts.

PEACH

Summer fruit of the plant *Prunus persica*, the peach is low in calories, rich in water, diuretic, easily digestible and, at times, slightly laxative. There are different varieties: white or yellow flesh, smooth or velvety skin. Fragrant and irresistible, it is ideal for making juices, smoothies and fruit salads, as well as exquisite desserts. Satiating and refreshing, it is highly recommended in a low-calorie diet. It contains calcium, potassium, phosphorus and flavonoids with antioxidant properties.

PEAR

This fruit can be found almost all year, although it actually ripens in the summer. If stored in a cool place it will keep for several weeks, preserving both its aroma and texture. It is low in calories, easily digestible and, thanks to the amount of lignin present, able to fight "bad" cholesterol. Due to its characteristics, it is suitable for eating cooked or for making refreshing smoothies, fruit salads, cakes and desserts.

In addition to being delicious, the plum is recognized for its digestive and laxative properties, as well as its ability to facilitate the elimination of uric acid, with consequent improvements in appearance and form. It can be found fresh in summer and fall; dried year-round. Fresh plums have a high water content, are low in calories and contain calcium, potassium, phosphorus and, among others, vitamins C, folic acid and retinol. Not recommended in the presence of colitis or abdominal cramps. Great to eat as they are or for making jams, juices and smoothies.

PLUM

GRAPES

The fruit of *Vitis vinifica* are recognized for their cleansing, detoxifying and diuretic properties. The berries, which can vary in size and color, are a valuable ally in our health and beauty. High-energy and antioxidant, grapes help regulate bowel movements. They ripen between summer and fall, and are also available in the form of raisins, known for their energy-boosting and sweetening properties. Fresh grapes have 61 calories per 100 grams (3.5 oz.), while dried ones have 283. Both contain minerals such as calcium, potassium and phosphorus, and above all vitamins A and C.

GOJI BERRIES

It seems that these little berries have anti-degenerative properties and are able to strengthen the immune system. They originate from the wild shrub *Lycium barbarum*, originally found in Mongolia, Tibet and the Himalayas, but for some years now they have been exported to enrich diets around the world. Extremely rich in vitamin C, they are nutritious energy-boosters (320 calories per 100 grams / 3.5 oz.). Experts recommend no more than 30 grams (1 oz.) per day. In the presence of diseases and medical care it is advisable to consult a specialist before including this food in your diet.

DATES

CHESTNUTS

The fruits of *Castanea sativa*, a plant belonging to the Fagacee family, chestnuts are high-energy, satiating and rich in starch, but they are gluten-free and therefore suitable for those with celiac disease. Chestnuts are rich in potassium, phosphorus, sulfur, magnesium and dietary fiber, promoting bowel movements, but are not recommended in the presence of colitis or abdominal bloating. They can be used in many dishes, both as a whole fruit or as flour. They have 189 calories per 100 grams (3.5 oz.).

Hazelnuts are a fruit with a woody shell, whose delicious seeds lend themselves to many sweet and savory recipes. Their nutritional characteristics make them a valuable ingredient in a balanced diet. They are high in lipids, protein, dietary fiber and minerals such as potassium, phosphorus, calcium, magnesium, iron, copper and selenium. Among the vitamins: B-group, A and E. High-energy and high-calorie, they have 625 calories per 100 grams (3.5 oz.).

HAZELNUTS

Dates are very important fruit, both for the components beneficial for our well-being and their use in cooking. They are naturally sweet, especially when dried, and thanks to their soft consistency are suitable for making delicious cakes, without having to add sugars. High-energy, 253 calories per 100 grams (3.5 oz.), they contain very little water and minerals such as calcium, potassium and phosphorus. Thanks to the dietary fiber, they promote bowel movements.

PINE NUTS

Oily seeds of the *Pinus pinea* species, pine nuts are high in fat, protein and carbohydrates. They are a true ally in our well-being, as they are able to provide energy in times of stress caused by studying or sports activities. They are rich in phosphorus and potassium, but also contain calcium, zinc and, among the vitamins, E, retinol and folic acid. Extremely high-calorie (567 calories per 100 grams / 3.5 oz.), they should be introduced into your diet with caution, especially if you are overweight.

DRIED FIGS

The dried fig is a high-energy fruit (270 calories per 100 grams / 3.5 oz.) and a valuable source of sugar, vitamins and minerals. Excellent when eaten in its natural form, it is also a wonderful ingredient if finely chopped and added to naturally sweet desserts (raw vegans included). Rich in mucilage and fiber, they are indicated for those suffering from irregular bowel movements. It appears that figs also improve the quality of the skin.

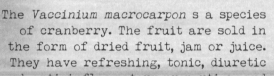

The *Vaccinium macrocarpon* s a species of cranberry. The fruit are sold in the form of dried fruit, jam or juice. They have refreshing, tonic, diuretic and anti-inflammatory properties, and appear to offer protection against free radical damage. They are a remedy that can be used to alleviate the symptoms of cystitis and can promote the balance of cholesterol, helping to lower "bad" levels. An ideal ingredient for desserts, bars and smoothies.

ALMONDS

Almonds are high-energy and rich in unsaturated fatty acids. They are said to slow down the aging process, which would make them a true ally to beauty. They are rich in vitamin E and folic acid, and contain important minerals such as calcium, phosphorus, potassium and zinc. Thanks to their fiber content they can help with irregular bowel movements. Great to eat on their own, almonds are also a fantastic ingredient for making refreshing energy-boosting beverages. Five almonds a day is the recommended amount to enjoy their benefits without negative consequences, due to their high calorie content.

Walnuts are a great help in the fight against high cholesterol and in reducing the damaging oxidative process in cells: the lipids in this fruit promote a healthy, radiant complexion. In fact, walnut oil is not only good in the kitchen, but also in cosmetics. Walnuts contain monounsaturated fatty acids, such as omega 3, which experts consider beneficial for preventing aging. They are high-calorie and therefore it's best not to overdo it: there are 660 calories in every 100 grams (3.5 oz.)!

WALNUTS

CRANBERRIES

PISTACHIOS

Pistachios are the seed of the *Pistacia vera* fruit, which belongs to the Anacardiaceae family. They contain mainly unsaturated fatty acids (omega 3 and omega 6), which can help to lower "bad" cholesterol and reduce the damaging oxidative process in cells. They contain tryptophan, which the body turns into serotonin, helping to improve our mood and help us sleep. Like all nuts they should be eaten in moderation, as they are high in calories (560 calories per 100 grams / 3.5 oz.), and it is preferable to buy them unsalted.

It is an excellent ingredient for desserts because its slightly sweet taste means that you can reduce the amount of sugar. It contains high amounts of proteins, lipids, glucides and minerals, which makes oat an important food for diets devoid of animal proteins. It is indicated for athletes and anyone, who due to work or studying, needs to concentrate for a long time. It is suitable for making delicious and satisfying cookies, cakes and creams. There are 390 calories per 100 grams (3.5 oz.).

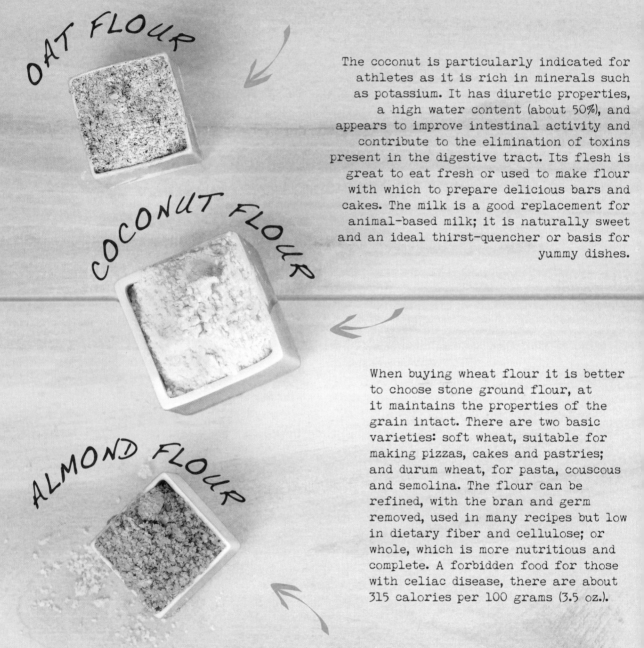

OAT FLOUR

COCONUT FLOUR

ALMOND FLOUR

The coconut is particularly indicated for athletes as it is rich in minerals such as potassium. It has diuretic properties, a high water content (about 50%), and appears to improve intestinal activity and contribute to the elimination of toxins present in the digestive tract. Its flesh is great to eat fresh or used to make flour with which to prepare delicious bars and cakes. The milk is a good replacement for animal-based milk; it is naturally sweet and an ideal thirst-quencher or basis for yummy dishes.

When buying wheat flour it is better to choose stone ground flour, at it maintains the properties of the grain intact. There are two basic varieties: soft wheat, suitable for making pizzas, cakes and pastries; and durum wheat, for pasta, couscous and semolina. The flour can be refined, with the bran and germ removed, used in many recipes but low in dietary fiber and cellulose; or whole, which is more nutritious and complete. A forbidden food for those with celiac disease, there are about 315 calories per 100 grams (3.5 oz.).

Making almond flour at home is extremely easy and highly recommended to obtain a product rich in nutrients. With a pestle or slow-speed grinder the dried seeds are transformed into a perfect flour for making delicious tasting cookies, creams and cakes, rich in elements beneficial for our well-being. Almond flour, blended with a glass of water, becomes an excellent mineralizing drink with energy-boosting properties.

Hazelnuts are fruits whose woody shell encases a crunchy and extremely nutritious seed: there are 625 calories per 100 grams (3.5 oz.), but their properties make it a food that should not to be overlooked. They contain proteins, lipids, fiber, minerals such as iron, calcium, potassium, phosphorus and zinc, and vitamins such as folic acid, retinol and E. The flour is excellent for making cakes with low sugar content. Hazelnuts can also be found in the form of oil.

HAZELNUT FLOUR

CAROB FLOUR

The carob belongs to the legume family and its fruit looks like a large woody pod. The seeds and pulp are used to produce flour with which to make desserts, ice creams and jams. Widely used as a thickener, the flour is used for making cakes that, due to their color and flavor, are similar to those made with cocoa. It contains minerals such as potassium, calcium and iron, fiber to promote bowel movements, and it is gluten-free: these are just some of its valuable properties.

COCOA

Cocoa powder is a key ingredient in many scrumptious and high-energy desserts. It consists of cocoa butter, sugars, proteins, fiber, minerals such as potassium, sodium, phosphorus, iron and zinc, and theobromine, a substance that stimulates the central nervous system. Cocoa-based foods are indicated for any situation that requires concentration and energy. There are about 355 calories per 100 grams (3.5 oz.).

WHEAT FLOUR

Linseeds are great for making refreshing decoctions or to enrich breads and focaccias. Good and beneficial, they are known for their soothing properties and ability to stimulate the digestive system and its functions: in fact they are considered an excellent remedy to combat constipation. It appears that they are also able to help the intestinal flora and strengthen the immune system. They are ideal freshly roasted to embellish salads, pasta and savory dishes in general.

LINSEEDS

CHIA SEEDS

Hugely successful small seeds thanks to the merits attributed to them: the sense of satiety, lowering "bad" cholesterol, omega 3 that slows down the aging process in our tissues. They most definitely taste good and do not contain gluten, so they are also suitable for people with celiac disease. Ideal for making breading for balls, as well as in salads, breads and savory snacks.

POPPY SEEDS

Like all oily seeds, they are rich in lipids, including polyunsaturated omega-6 fatty acids. They are high calorie (525 calories per 100 grams / 3.5 oz.), but thanks to their strong flavor and nutty character a few teaspoons are enough to enrich sweet and savory recipes. Excellent for embellishing salads, especially those of blanched or steamed vegetables, they are a valuable source of minerals like manganese, calcium, copper, selenium and phosphorus, as well as B-group vitamins and vitamins C and E.

BLACK SESAME SEEDS

According to Chinese medicine, this little black seed is an ally of the kidneys and liver, and, contrary to its white counterpart (beneficial when treating the same organs), it is effective in preventing diseases. It is considered a valuable food to help counter the effects of aging: it is said that it can reduce annoying ringing in the ears, and even that is the symbol of immortality! But aside from these interesting tidbits, the black sesame is rich in calcium, zinc, magnesium and vitamins. The oil content helps lubricate the intestines and, thanks to fiber, to regulate bowel movements.

SUNFLOWER SEEDS

Sunflower oil is very well-known, but the seeds themselves can be an important part of a diet because they are rich in nutrients beneficial for our well-being. They contain many minerals, such as iron, manganese, zinc, potassium, phosphorus, calcium and, above all, folic acid and vitamin E, all properties that make it a good everyday food. They enrich bread, cookies, cakes and salads and, given their exquisite taste, it is a true pleasure to include them in your diet.

HEMP SEEDS

Considered a superfood, they are rich in valuable properties: anti-inflammatory and natural anti-oxidants, they can strengthen the nervous system, helping to counter "bad" cholesterol and reduce the effects of aging. They also contain minerals such as iron, calcium, magnesium, potassium and phosphorus, and several vitamins, E, A, B1, B2, PP and C. They are an ideal ingredient for enriching dishes based on legumes, carbohydrates and vegetables. You can make a delicious polenta by mixing hemp seed flour with corn flour.

WHITE SESAME SEEDS

Rich in lipids, these small seeds are high calorie (approximately 600 calories per 100 grams / 3.5 oz.) and an excellent source of calcium, zinc, selenium, phosphorus, potassium and magnesium. They also contain proteins and vitamins such as A and B6. They will enrich any sweet or savory recipe. They taste great and are a food to be reckoned with in any diet, but especially in those that are devoid of animal protein.

PUMPKIN SEEDS

It appears that pumpkin seeds are a valuable ally for the heart, good moods and sleeping well at night. They are very tasty and will embellish any dish, especially savory ones. A source of important minerals such as iron, zinc and magnesium, they can help regulate your cholesterol level, counteract loss of energy and combat inflammation, irritation and swelling. They have 445 calories per 100 grams (3.5 oz.).

With Grains...

Grains are the fruit of herbaceous plants in the grass family and are one of the pillars of human nutrition. The list includes wheat, rice, barley, oat, maize, millet and buckwheat, although the latter belongs to the Polygonaceae family. Some are rich in gluten, such as wheat, others are not, such as millet, and are therefore suitable for the diets of those with celiac disease. We can find them in the form of groats, flour, beverages and creams, whole or refined, and they are ideal for the creation of many sweet, savory, moist or dry dishes. Grains contain water (about 10-12%), proteins (from 8% in oat to 13% in durum wheat), a high amount of carbohydrates (up to 87% in white rice), fibers (especially in unrefined grains) and are low-fat (almost absent in polished white rice, and up to 7% in oat). All grains are a great source of energy and when combined with legumes they can easily replace animal proteins. Ideally it is best to limit refined grains as much as possible, favoring the groats or freshly ground flours.

Cream of Oats with Vegetables

Servings

3.5 oz. (100 g) oat flakes – 1 pt. (5 dl) vegetable stock – 2 carrots – 2 zucchini – 2 small peppers – 1 bunch of aromatic herbs: oregano, rosemary, marjoram – 2 tbsp (20 g) extra virgin olive oil – salt – pepper

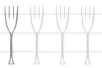

Difficulty

1. Wash and trim the vegetables, then chop into small pieces.

2. Heat the oil and add the herbs; remove them when the oil is aromatized. Add the vegetables and cook for 7-10 minutes, adding salt and pepper to taste, and a few tablespoons of hot water so that the vegetables do not dry out and burn.

3. Bring the stock to the boil and add the oats. Stir well, adding salt and pepper to taste, and after 2 minutes remove from the heat.

4. Add the vegetables to the cream of oats and serve.

Prep Time
5 minutes

Cooking Time
10 minutes

Barley and Bean Salad

Servings

3.5 oz. (100 g) barley - 7 oz. (200 g) boiled beans of your choice - 1 scallion - 2 small sweet peppers - 2 fresh medium-hot chili peppers - 1 lime - 4 tbsp (40 g) extra virgin olive oil - salt

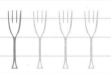

Difficulty

**Prep Time
10 minutes**

**Cooking Time
30 minutes**

1. Wash the barley and boil in salted water for 30 minutes. Check that the consistency is to your taste and then drain. Dress immediately with 2 tablespoons of oil so that the groats don't stick together; add the drained beans.

2. Peel and slice the scallion. Wash and dry the peppers and chili peppers, and cut them into pieces, removing the seeds first. Add all the ingredients to the salad.

3. Squeeze the lime (keep two slices to decorate), and add it to the other ingredients, stir well, and pour over the remaining oil; salt to taste and then serve.

Chestnut Bread with Figs and Chili

Servings

2 cups (200 g) buckwheat flour – 1 cup (100 g) chestnut flour – 4 tbsp (40 g) extra virgin olive oil or hazelnut oil – 1 oz. (30 g) pine nuts – 8 dried figs – 2 hot, dried chili peppers of your choice – 1.5 tsp (5 g) yeast for savory dishes – salt – rosemary

Difficulty

1. Mix the yeast in 5 fl oz. (1.5 dl) of warm water. Crumble the chili peppers. Cut the figs into pieces.

2. Mix the flours, add the oil, salt, water with the yeast, and knead until you get a smooth and sticky dough without any lumps. Add a few more tablespoons of water if necessary. Sprinkle your hands with oil every now and then to facilitate kneading. Add half of the figs, pine nuts and chili pepper. Leave to rise in a warm place for at least one hour.

**Prep Time
20 minutes**

3. Pre-heat the oven to 350 degrees F (180 degrees C), line a loaf pan with wax paper and transfer the dough; decorate with the left-over ingredients and the rosemary, and put in the oven.

**Cooking Time
40 minutes**

4. Bake for 10 minutes, then lower the temperature by 50 degrees F (10 degrees C) and bake for a further 25 minutes. Take the pan out of the oven, turn the loaf over and put it back in the oven for another five minutes. Remove from the oven and leave to cool before cutting.

Vegetable Wholegrain Bread with Mandarin Orange Salad

Servings

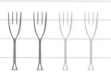

Difficulty

Prep Time
20 minutes

Cooking Time
50 minutes

For the bread: 3 cups (300 g) self-rising wholemeal flour – 2 purple carrots – 1 zucchini
For the salad: 1 head of lettuce – 2 mandarins – 1 orange – 4 purple carrots – 1 fresh red chili pepper – 2.5 tbsp (20 g) pistachios – 4 tbsp (40 g) mix of linseed, hemp and extra virgin olive oil – 12 basil leaves – salt

1. Pre-heat the oven to 320 degrees F (160 degrees C). Wash the vegetables for the bread and cut them into strips. Roll out the dough on a floured work surface, distribute the vegetables and roll them inside the dough; leave to rise in a warm place for 30 minutes.

2. Put in the oven and bake for 40 minutes; take out of the oven and turn the loaf over, then cook for a further 10 minutes. When cooked, take the loaf out of the oven and leave to cool.

3. Trim, wash, dry and chop the lettuce. Peel the mandarins and the orange, dice them and put them in the bowl. Peel the carrots and cut into pieces; add to the lettuce together with the chili pepper, chopped at the last moment, pistachios and basil leaves.

4. Dress with oil and salt to taste, mix and serve with the bread.

Wholegrain Bread with Sun-dried Tomatoes and Olives

Servings

2 1/2 cups (250 g) wholemeal flour - 1/2 cup (50 g) oat flour - 4 tbsp (40 g) extra virgin olive oil - 10 sun-dried tomatoes - 20 pitted olives in brine - 1.5 tsp (5 g) yeast for savory dishes - salt

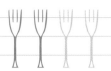

Difficulty

Prep Time
20 minutes

Cooking Time
40 minutes

1. Pre-heat the oven to 350 degrees F (180 degrees C). Soak the tomatoes in warm water for 5 minutes, then drain them and cut them into small pieces. Drain and chop the olives.

2. Dissolve the yeast in a glass of warm water. Put the flour into a bowl, add the oil and the water with the yeast and mix together. Knead the mixture until it is smooth, lump-free and shiny. If necessary add another few tablespoons of warm water, until you get a firm yet very soft dough.

3. Add the tomatoes, olives and salt to taste; knead again and leave to rise in a warm place for 2 hours. Then divide the dough into pieces and shape them as you like; leave to rise for a further 30 minutes before baking.

4. Cook for 10 minutes at 350 degrees F (180 degrees C) and then lower to 320 degrees F (160 degrees C) for about 30 minutes. Check that the rolls are cooked on the inside (pierce with a cocktail stick; it should come out clean). When they are cooked, take out of the oven and leave to cool before serving.

Semolina and Millet Polenta

Servings

For the polenta: 3.5 oz. (100 g) durum semolina - 2 oz. (50 g) millet flour- 2 oz. (50 g) corn flour - 3.5 fl oz. (1 dl) soya milk - 1 tsp chopped lemon rind - 10 tbsp (100 g) peanut oil - salt - pepper
For the cream: 3.5 oz. (100 g) oat cream - coarse pepper to taste - 1 dried hot chili pepper - salt

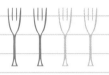

Difficulty

1. Mix the flours in a good-sized saucepan (keeping half of the corn and millet flours aside for the breading); stir in the milk and lemon rind and mix well, adding a little water at a time so that the mixture remains soft. Add salt and pepper to taste.

2. Continue stirring, bring to the boil over a low flame and, after one minute, remove from the heat and pour onto a suitable surface to cool down.

Prep Time 20 minutes

3. In the meantime, finely chop the chili pepper and mix it with 4-5 ground pepper corns and salt to taste; season the oat cream.

4. When the polenta is firm and cold, cut into pieces, coat in the left-over flour and fry in very hot oil.

Cooking Time 10 minutes

5. Serve the polenta on skewers and with the sauce at room temperature.

Quinoa and Brown Rice Balls

Servings

2.5 oz. (75 g) quinoa, boiled and drained – 3.5 oz. (100 g) brown rice, boiled and drained – 1 oz. (30 g) soy cream – 1 oz. (30 g) linseeds – 1 oz. (30 g) sunflower seeds – 2 oz. (50 g) breadcrumbs – 1 tsp curry powder – 10 tbsp (100 g) sunflower oil – salt

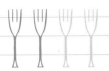

Difficulty

1. Prepare the breading by pouring the linseeds into a flat dish together with the breadcrumbs; mix well.

2. Put the quinoa and rice in a bowl and add the soy cream, curry powder, sunflower seeds and salt to taste. Hand roll into small, round balls and cover with the breading.

**Prep Time
20 minutes**

3. Heat the oil and when really hot add the quinoa balls. Let the oil seal the balls well before turning them (about 2-3 minutes) and when they're an even golden color drain and leave to dry on kitchen paper.

4. Serve hot, if you prefer you can serve them with a tomato sauce or cream of cereal grains.

**Cooking Time
10 minutes**

Brown and Red Rice with Crunchy Vegetables and Paprika Cream

Servings

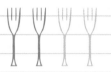

Difficulty

Prep Time
20 minutes

Cooking Time
30 minutes

For the base: 3.5 oz. (100 g) brown rice – 3.5 oz. (100 g) red rice – 3.5 oz. (100 g) vegetable cream – 3 tbsp (30 g) – extra virgin olive oil – 12 basil leaves, washed and dried – 1 tsp paprika – salt and pepper
For the decoration: 1 carrot – 1 zucchini – rind of half an orange

1. Pre-heat the oven to 390 degrees F (200 degrees C). Cut the vegetables and orange rind into strips and stir-fry.

2. Wash the two types of rice separately and boil covered, still separately, for 10 minutes in double their volume of water. Turn off and leave to stand for 30 minutes, after which the grains should be cooked and the water completely absorbed.

3. Put the red rice in a bowl and season with oil, and salt and pepper to taste. Put the brown rice in another bowl and add the cream, paprika and salt and pepper to taste. Mix well.

4. When preparing the food on the plate, use a ring to help you: create the first layer with white rice, decorate with 3 basil leaves and add a second layer of red rice.

5. Decorate with the crunchy vegetables and serve.

Brown Rice Risotto with Cabbage, Scallions and Sprouts

Servings

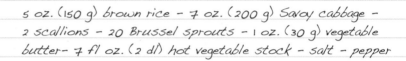

5 oz. (150 g) brown rice - 7 oz. (200 g) Savoy cabbage - 2 scallions - 20 Brussel sprouts - 1 oz. (30 g) vegetable butter - 7 fl oz. (2 dl) hot vegetable stock - salt - pepper

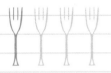

Difficulty

Prep Time
10 minutes

Cooking Time
20 minutes

1. Wash the rice and boil it covered for 10 minutes, in twice its volume of water, over a low heat. Turn off and leave to stand for 30 minutes.

2. Trim, wash and cut the Brussels sprouts into two or four pieces, depending on the size. Trim the cabbage and cut into strips. Peel the scallions and slice finely.

3. Melt half the butter in a non-stick pan, brown the scallions and add the Brussel sprouts and cabbage. Cook for 5 minutes, adding a few tablespoons of stock when necessary.

4. When the vegetables are the right consistency for your taste, add the well-drained rice. Add salt, stir, add the left-over butter and sauté to blend the flavors. Add more stock if necessary.

5. Serve the risotto hot, and if you like add a generous amount of ground pepper.

Seitan with Vegetables

Servings

2 cups (300 g) seitan - half an eggplant - 2 leeks -
2 carrots - 1 small Chinese cabbage - 5 tbsp (50 g) peanut
or corn oil - 3 tbsp (30 g) extra virgin olive oil -
salt - pepper

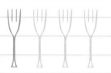

Difficulty

1. Cut the eggplant into small cubes, place them on a chopping board and sprinkle with a pinch of salt to draw out the moisture, then rinse and dry. Wash all the other ingredients and cut them into small pieces.

2. First cook the eggplants in very hot oil. When they are golden, drain them and wipe off the excess oil with kitchen roll. Cook the other vegetables in the same way, one type at a time. Mix them all together in a bowl.

Prep Time
10 minutes

3. Pour a thin layer of olive oil into a frying pan and add the sliced seitan together with the vegetables: add salt and pepper to taste, two tablespoons of hot water and stir; as soon as the water has evaporated, remove from the heat and serve.

Cooking Time
20 minutes

Turmeric Tagliolini with Asparagus

Servings

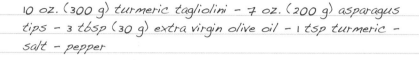

10 oz. (300 g) turmeric tagliolini – 7 oz. (200 g) asparagus tips – 3 tbsp (30 g) extra virgin olive oil – 1 tsp turmeric – salt – pepper

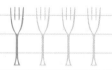

Difficulty

Prep Time
5 minutes

Cooking Time
20 minutes

1. Wash the asparagus tips and cut them into rounds. Pour the oil into a non-stick pan and, when hot, add the asparagus. Cook for about 10 minutes or until they reach the desired consistency, adding a few tablespoons of hot water when necessary.

2. Add the turmeric at the last minute, dissolved in a tablespoon of hot water, mix in and turn off the heat.

3. Boil the tagliolini in boiling salted water. When al dente, drain and add to the condiment. Mix gently and leave on the heat for half a minute, adding a couple of tablespoons of cooking water from the pasta and a sprinkling of pepper.

4. Serve immediately.

Spicy Wheat Berry Pie with Vegetables

Servings

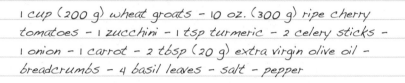

1 cup (200 g) wheat groats - 10 oz. (300 g) ripe cherry tomatoes - 1 zucchini - 1 tsp turmeric - 2 celery sticks - 1 onion - 1 carrot - 2 tbsp (20 g) extra virgin olive oil - breadcrumbs - 4 basil leaves - salt - pepper

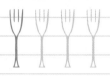

Difficulty

1. Prepare the vegetable stock by chopping the celery, carrot and onion, and cooking them in four pints (two liters) of water. Let it evaporate by half, strain and put the stock back in the pan.

2. Wash the wheat and cook it in the stock for 40 minutes. Drain, keeping half a glass of stock for dissolving the turmeric.

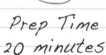

Prep Time
20 minutes

3. Pre-heat the oven to 390 degrees F (200 degrees C). Wash the vegetables, cut the cherry tomatoes in half and the zucchini into strips. Grease the baking tray with the oil, add the wheat together with the vegetables and pour the turmeric over the top. Salt and pepper to taste, sprinkle with the breadcrumbs and bake in the oven for 20 minutes.

Cooking Time
60 minutes

4. Take out of the oven when cooked, add the fresh basil and serve.

Whole Wheat, Bulgur and Escarole Pie

Servings

Difficulty

Prep Time
20 minutes

Cooking Time
35 minutes

2 cups (200 g) wheat grains, already cooked – 1 cup (100 g) bulgur – 3.5 oz. (100 g) large leafed escarole – 3.5 oz. (100 g) smoked tofu – 2 carrots – 1 scallion – 2 oz. (50 g) soy cream – 2 tbsp (20 g) breadcrumbs – 1 sachet of saffron – 2 tbsp (20 g) extra virgin olive oil – salt

1. Wash the lettuce and dry carefully. Cook the bulgur covered for 10 minutes, in twice its volume of water; turn off and leave to stand for 30 minutes.

2. Wash the carrots and chop them together with the scallion. Also cut the tofu. Dissolve the saffron in the soy cream.

3. Pre-heat the oven to 390 degrees F (200 degrees C). Mix the wheat and the bulgur together, add the vegetables and the cream, salt to taste. Grease the bottom and sides of a baking tray and line with the escarole leaves, fill with the wheat mixture.

4. Sprinkle the top with the breadcrumbs. Bake the pie for 20–25 minutes, then remove from the oven. Leave to cool for a few minutes and serve.

With Legumes...

Although important in any diet, legumes are even more so in a vegan one, as they are rich in proteins and can replace those of animal origin. They taste really good and there are many varieties to choose from to create minestrones, salads, soups, pies and anything else that takes your fancy. The abundant and diverse family of legumes includes peas, beans, lentils, soybeans, fava beans and chickling peas. Between them there are so many different colors and sizes, that you can, if you wish, eat something different every day! Large, chunky beans are great for making wonderful salads, in particular the Lima variety, as they retain their shape during cooking. With fava beans you can make sauces and purees, soups with lentils, jams with Azuki; the list is endless. They can be found fresh in summer and dry year-round, the latter of which should first be soaked for about ten hours, so as to facilitate cooking. They help the digestive system due to the fibers, and contrary to what you may think, they are not fattening; actually, they absorb liquids and leave a pleasant feeling of satiety.

Black Chickpeas with Brown Rice and Herbs

Servings

5 oz. (150 g) black chickpeas - 5 oz. (150 g) brown rice -
1 tbsp chopped aromatic herbs: rosemary, thyme, oregano -
1 scallion - 1 carrot - 2 celery sticks - 4 tbsp (40 g)
extra virgin olive oil - 1 tbsp Umeboshi vinegar -
salt - pepper

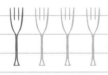

Difficulty

1. Soak the chickpeas for about 8-10 hours, changing the water a few times; drain and wash. Boil them in about 2 pints (1 liter) of salted water together with the whole vegetables, which have been washed. Leave to cook for about 2 hours, stirring every now and then.

2. Once cooked, drain the chickpeas, add salt and dress with two tablespoons of oil. Blend the vegetables with the stock and put to one side.

**Prep Time
10 minutes**

3. In the meantime, wash the rice and boil it, covered, for about 30 minutes; drain and dress with two tablespoons of oil and one of Umeboshi vinegar.

4. Put the dish together by layering the rice and chickpeas. Dress with one tablespoon of stock and serve at the table with oil, pepper and a sprinkling of aromatic herbs.

**Cooking Time
120 minutes**

Cream of Chickpea with Azuki Beans and Wild Rice

Servings

7 oz. (200 g) soaked white chickpeas – 1 zucchini –
3.5 oz. (100 g) broccoli – 1/2 cup (50 g) wild rice –
2 oz. (50 g) soaked Azuki – 2 bay leaves – 4 tbsp (40 g)
extra virgin olive oil – 4 fresh chili peppers – salt

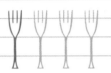

Difficulty

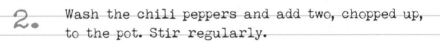

1. Boil the chickpeas and Azuki beans in 2 pints (1 liter) of water, together with the bay leaves, zucchini and broccoli. Regulate the heat to ensure that the stock doesn't evaporate too much during the 2 hours needed to cook the legumes.

2. Wash the chili peppers and add two, chopped up, to the pot. Stir regularly.

3. Add the rice after 90 minutes. If the soup looks too dry, add a ladle or two of boiling water. Cook for a further 30 minutes and when the rice is cooked season with the remaining chili pepper, oil, salt to taste; serve while hot.

Prep Time
10 minutes

Cooking Time
120 minutes

Lentils with Cherry Tomatoes and Tofu

Servings

2 cups (200 g) lentils – 1 scallion – 7 oz. (200 g) cherry tomatoes – 1 zucchini – 2 carrots – 2 celery sticks – 2 fresh hot chili peppers – 3.5 oz. (100 g) smoked tofu – 2 tbsp (20 g) extra virgin olive oil – 2 tbsp (about 20 g) linseed oil – 4 tbsp (40 g) freshly squeezed lemon juice – salt

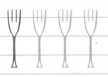

Difficulty

1. Wash the celery, one carrot and the scallion; put them into a pot with 2 pints (1 liter) of water and boil. Once the vegetable stock is ready, add the lentils and cook for about 1 hour. The cooking time is halved if the lentils are first soaked in cold water for 4-5 hours.

Prep Time
20 minutes

2. While the legumes are cooking, prepare the condiment: cut the remaining carrot and the zucchini into long thin strips; the cherry tomatoes into two or four parts, depending on the size; and the tofu into small pieces. Put all of the ingredients into a large soup bowl.

3. Drain the lentils and add them to the condiment; season with sliced chili pepper, oil, lemon juice, salt to taste, and mix well. You can serve the dish while it is still hot, but it is also tasty at room temperature.

Cooking Time
60 minutes

Mixed Legumes with Purple Potatoes, Mushrooms and Artichokes

Servings

4 purple potatoes - 4 artichokes - 1 cup (100 g) tomato sauce - 1 lb. (400 g) boiled mixed legumes: Borlotti and Lima beans, white chickpeas, green soybeans - 7 oz. (200 g) fresh mushrooms (e.g. cardoncelli) - 4 tbsp (40 g) extra virgin olive oil - 2 tbsp (20 g) apple vinegar - 2 bay leaves - salt - chili to taste

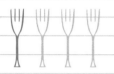

Difficulty

1. Steam the potatoes. Remove from the heat after about 30 minutes; peel and slice them.

2. Trim and wash the artichokes; cook them in water with two tablespoons of vinegar for 10 minutes, then drain.

3. Trim the mushrooms, removing the end of the stalks, and slice them. Cook for 5 minutes with one tablespoon of oil, the bay leaves and the tomato sauce.

Prep Time
20 minutes

4. Mix the mushrooms with the legumes and artichokes; dress with the left-over oil. Add the potatoes, divide into portions and serve with the chili pepper on the side.

Cooking Time
30 minutes

Whole Wheat Penne Pasta in Mixed Legume Soup

Servings

7 oz. (200 g) mixed legumes of your choice, already soaked – 2 oz. (50 g) fresh soybeans – 10 oz. (300 g) peeled tomatoes – 2 tbsp (20 g) extra virgin olive oil – 1 finely chopped onion – 10 oz. (300 g) whole wheat penne – salt – pepper

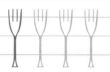

Difficulty

1. Put the legumes, peeled tomatoes, onion and oil in a high-sided pan. Mix the ingredients together and cook over a low heat for about 90 minutes, checking regularly and adding a ladle of boiling water every now and then to ensure that there is always liquid.

2. Add salt and pepper to taste. Add the fresh soybeans and cook for about another 20 minutes.

Prep Time
10 minutes

3. Boil the pasta in another pan, in a large quantity of water. When it is al dente, transfer it to the pan with the legumes and stir in. Boil over a high heat for one minute.

4. You can serve the penne with or without the cooking stock. Either way it is a delicious pasta dish.

Cooking Time
120 minutes

Herby Peas with White Rice, Jalapeño and Seaweed

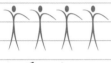

Servings

For the rice: 1 cup (200 g) white rice – 1.5 tsp (5 g) Dulse seaweed – 1 jalapeño chili pepper – 1 lemon – 2 tbsp (20 g) oil, half linseed and half hemp
For the peas: 10 oz. (300 g) fresh green peas – 2 oz. (50 g) dried wild peas – 1 sprig of rosemary, 2 of thyme, 2 of marjoram – 2 cloves of garlic – 2 tbsp (20 g) oil, half linseed and half hemp – salt

Difficulty

1. Soak the dried peas for at least 10 hours, changing the water as often as possible, and then boil them for about 2 hours. Drain and transfer them to a pan with two tablespoons of oil.

2. Trim and finely chop the aromatic herbs. Put them in the pan together with the garlic and green peas, salt, stir and then cook over a low heat. Cook the legumes for about 10 minutes, adding a few tablespoons of hot water if necessary.

Prep Time
10 minutes

3. In the meantime, wash the white rice thoroughly and then boil it in twice its volume of water, covered, for about 8 minutes; switch off and let the water absorb completely. Dress with the left-over oil, the seaweed, after having soaked it for two minutes and drained well, the freshly cut jalapeño and a few drops of lemon juice.

Cooking Time
130 minutes

4. Serve the rice and peas separately and eat as desired.

Fava Bean Puree

Servings

5 oz. (150 g) dried fava beans – 2 scallions – 1 clove of garlic – 1 tsp chopped aromatic herbs: rosemary, oregano, marjoram – 1 tbsp mixed spice powder: paprika, cumin, cardamom, coriander, turmeric – 4 tbsp (40 g) extra virgin olive oil – salt – 4 wheat flour tortillas to serve with the puree

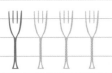

Difficulty

1. Soak the fava beans in water and leave them to soften for about 6-10 hours. Wash them and boil in 2 pints (1 liter) of water, adding the garlic, the peeled and finely chopped scallions, and the aromatic herbs. Cook over a medium flame, stirring regularly.

**Prep Time
15 minutes**

2. When the legumes start to split (about 30-40 minutes), make sure that most of the water has evaporated and then add the spices and salt to taste; blend and thicken the legumes. If the cream is too runny, leave it over the heat for a few more minutes. When it has reached the right consistency, add the oil.

3. Transfer the puree onto the plates, decorate as you like and serve with the tortillas.

**Cooking Time
30-40
minutes**

Green Soybeans in Tomato Sauce with Hemp Seed Rice Balls

Servings

7 oz. (200 g) soybeans - 3.5 fl oz. (1 dl) vegetable stock - 1 tbsp tomato puree - 2 cups (200 g) cooked brown rice - 3.5 oz. (100 g) tofu - 2 oz. (50 g) cream of oat - 2 oz. (50 g) hemp seeds - 10 tbsp (100 g) peanut oil - salt - pepper

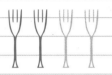

Difficulty

1. Dissolve the tomato puree in the stock and cook the soybeans. Stir every now and then and make sure that the stock doesn't disappear completely; if necessary add a few tablespoons of boiling water. Add salt and pepper to taste.

2. Meanwhile finely chop the tofu; mix it into the rice together with the cream of oat, and salt and pepper to taste. With damp hands (so that the mixture doesn't stick to them) make the rice balls as small or as big as you like.

Prep Time 20 minutes

3. Pour the hemp seeds onto a flat plate and roll the balls to cover them.

4. Heat the oil and add the rice balls. Wait until they are firm before turning them over (about 2-3 minutes). When they are an even golden color, remove them from the pan, drain and dry off the excess oil with kitchen roll.

Cooking Time 20 minutes

5. Serve the soybeans in tomato sauce and rice balls hot.

Red Soy Stew with Beans and Chili

Servings

4 rice tortillas - 5 oz. (150 g) soya chunks - 7 oz. (200 g) tomato sauce - 2 fresh medium-hot chili peppers - 7 oz. (200 g) fresh kidney beans - salt

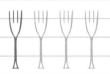

Difficulty

**Prep Time
20 minutes**

**Cooking Time
35 minutes**

1. Boil the beans in 2 pints (1 liter) of water for about 20 minutes, and then check the consistency: if they are soft, drain them and use the cooking water to rehydrate the soya chunks.

2. Boil the chunks for 10 minutes and then drain them; transfer to a pan together with the beans and tomato sauce, stir and leave to simmer for 5 minutes.

3. Chop the chili peppers and add to the pan, salt to taste and, when the tomato sauce has reduced by half, remove from the heat and serve the stew on the heated tortillas.

Smoked Tofu Roll with Chili and Spices

Servings

5 oz. (150 g) rolled smoked tofu, cut into slices -
2 fresh red chili peppers - 1 tbsp mixed spices: coriander
and cardamom - 2 tbsp (20 g) extra virgin olive oil -
2 tbsp (20 g) tamari sauce

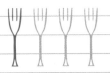

Difficulty

**Prep Time
5 minutes**

**Cooking Time
5 minutes**

1. Tofu that is already rolled and smoked is ideal for preparing sauces for pasta, rice etc. Its smokiness also adds an intense and delicious flavor to dishes. You can cut it into chunks or, once unrolled, into tiny pieces or long thin strips.

2. Pour the oil into a pan; add the spices, slightly crushed in a mortar, chopped chili peppers and the slices of tofu.

3. Cook over a medium-high flame for 3-4 minutes, just enough time to sauté the slices and fill the kitchen with wonderful smells.

4. Remove from the heat, moisten with the tamari sauce and serve.

Chickling Pea Soup with Wholegrain Spelt Linguine Pasta

Servings

7 oz. (200 g) chickling peas - 3.5 oz. (100 g) wholegrain spelt linguine pasta - 10 sun-dried tomatoes - 1 dried chili pepper - 2 cloves of garlic - 2 tbsp (20 g) extra virgin olive oil - salt - aromatic herbs: sage and rosemary

Difficulty

Prep Time
10 minutes

Cooking Time
130 minutes

1. Soak the chickling peas in cold water and leave for 24 to 48 hours, changing the water a few times.

2. Once ready, wash the peas and boil them in 2 pints (1 liter) of water, together with the garlic, crumbled chili pepper and half of the aromatic herbs, closed inside a net bag so that they can be easily removed.

3. Cook for 2 hours, then remove the bag of herbs and salt to taste. Break the linguine, chop the tomatoes and add to the pot with the chickling peas.

4. When the pasta is cooked, add two tablespoons of oil, mix and serve, decorating the dishes with the remaining herbs.

Wild Pea Soup with Potato Gnocchi

Servings

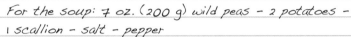

For the soup: 7 oz. (200 g) wild peas - 2 potatoes - 1 scallion - salt - pepper
For the gnocchi: 4 medium potatoes - 1 cup (100 g) white flour - 2 tbsp (20 g) extra virgin olive oil - salt

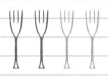

Difficulty

**Prep Time
60 minutes**

**Cooking Time
120 minutes**

1. Soak the peas for a day, changing the water as often as possible. Drain and put them in a pot with the two peeled potatoes, sliced scallion and about 2 pints (1 liter) of water. Leave to cook, checking every now and then that there is enough water and adding more when necessary.

2. In the meantime, prepare the gnocchi. Steam cook the four potatoes for about 30 minutes and then mash them. Mix with the flour, without kneading, and then make long sausages; cut the gnocchi as small or as big as you like. Leave on a floured baking tray until you're ready to use them.

3. When the pea soup is cooked (about 2 hours), mash any of the potato that is still intact and reduce the stock over a high heat. Add salt and pepper to taste.

4. Boil the gnocchi in salted water, just enough time for them to rise to the surface. Drain and drizzle them with oil; serve them together with the soup.

5. If you prefer, you can season with freshly ground pepper.

With Vegetables...

There are loads of different vegetables in each season, colorful, inviting, fragrant, versatile. Each month has its own distinct flavors and consistencies: summer vegetables are refreshing, rich in water and thirst-quenching, while winter veg are more solid and firm. They also form the basis of a balanced diet and an inexhaustible source of vitamins, minerals, fiber... true allies in our well-being! For every meal of the day you can create multicolored salads, with wild or cultivated chicory, brightly colored root vegetables, irresistible tomatoes, tiny and firm or large and juicy; with filling leaves such as cabbage or sheets of dried seaweed. Nature has myriad varieties to offers us year-round and there are infinite ways to use them: in crudités, in minestrones or soups, stewed or sautéed, alone or combined with grains and legumes.

Vegetables are a key resource for our nutrition and, for those who aren't particularly fond of them in their natural form, they are also fantastic for making juices and smoothies.

Garlic, Olives and Broccoli
with Spirulina Spaghetti

Servings

350 g whole grain spirulina spaghetti - 3.5 oz. (100 g)
broccoli - 20 pitted olives - 2 oz. (50 g) tofu -
4 cloves of garlic - 4 tbsp (40 g) extra virgin olive oil
20 cherry tomatoes - salt

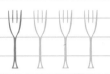

Difficulty

Prep Time
10 minutes

Cooking Time
15 minutes

1. Wash the broccoli and break into pieces. Cut the olives into rounds, wash the cherry tomatoes and cut them into two or four parts, depending on the size. Dice the tofu, peel and slice the garlic.

2. Bring the water for the pasta to the boil. In the meantime, pour two tablespoons of oil into a non-stick pan and delicately sauté the garlic so that it changes color without burning. Add the cherry tomatoes, olives, tofu and broccoli.

3. Leave to cook over a high flame for 5-7 minutes, mixing all the time, and then turn off.

4. Cook the spaghetti using the cooking time indicated on the packet; drain and transfer to the condiment, add the two left-over tablespoons of oil, salt and mix; serve immediately.

Cream of Zucchini with Kombu and Miso

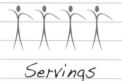

Servings

Difficulty

Prep Time
10 minutes

Cooking Time
30-40 minutes

4 zucchini - 2 potatoes - 1 onion - 1 piece of Kombu seaweed (about 2-3 g) - 2 tbsp Miso

1. Wash the zucchini, peel the onion and potatoes, and chop all of them into small pieces. Cook them together with the seaweed in 2 pints (1 liter) of water and, when the liquid has reduced by half, blend the soup.

2. If after about 30 minutes cooking the cream is thick enough, remove from the heat, or leave for another 5-10 minutes, stirring regularly.

3. Leave to cool until it reaches about 140 degrees F (60 degrees C) and then add the Miso. Stir until it is mixed well into the other ingredients.

4. Miso shouldn't be cooked or added to soups or creams that are too hot, otherwise its valuable characteristics may be ruined. Very salty and strong flavored, it makes soups just that little more tasty and appetizing.

Pumpkin and Poppy Seed Croissant

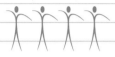

Servings

For the croissant: 7 oz. (200 g) vegan puff pastry - 2 oz. (50 g) tofu - 2 tbsp (30 g) pumpkin seeds - 2 tbsp (10 g) poppy seeds - salt - pepper
For the filling: 7 oz. (200 g) cardoncelli mushrooms - 2 cloves of garlic - 2 tbsp (20 g) extra virgin olive oil - 2 tbsp (20 g) tomato puree - salt - pepper

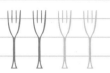

Difficulty

1. Prepare the sauce first. Trim, wash and dry the mushrooms, then slice them. Pour the oil into a saucepan and add the garlic, tomato puree and mushrooms; dilute with 3-4 tablespoons of hot water. Leave to cook for 5 minutes, salt and pepper to taste, remove the garlic and leave to cool.

**Prep Time
20 minutes**

2. Cut the tofu into pieces and mix them into the mushroom sauce together with the pumpkin seeds. If you like, you can season with salt and pepper to taste.

3. Pre-heat the oven to 390 degrees F (200 degrees C). Put the pastry on a suitable work surface and cover with baking paper. Cut the pastry into 4 parts, evenly distribute the filling and close the pastry, creating a shape of your choice; cover with poppy seeds. Transfer onto a baking tray lined with wax paper and put in the oven.

**Cooking Time
25 minutes**

4. Leave to cook for about 20 minutes, and when the pastry turns slightly golden take them out of the oven.

5. Leave them to cool down a little before serving.

Broccoli, Potato and Scallion Salad with Paprika Cream

Servings

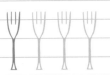

Difficulty

Prep Time
5 minutes

Cooking Time
30 minutes

4 yellow potatoes - 4 purple potatoes - 4 scallions - 1 lb. (400 g) broccoli - 7 oz. (200 g) vegetable cream - 3.5 oz. (100 g) avocado - 1 tsp paprika - salt - pepper

1. Wash and peel the potatoes, wash the broccoli and peel the scallions. Steam the vegetables: after about 10 minutes remove the broccoli and leave the rest of the vegetables in the pot.

2. After about 20 minutes check if the potatoes are soft; drain all of the vegetables and put them in a bowl.

3. Puree the avocado flesh, add the paprika, salt and pepper, then the cream; whisk with an electric whisk for 2 minutes and serve with the vegetables.

Fermented Cabbage, Daikon and Carrot

500 g Jar

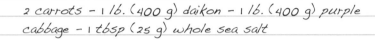

2 carrots – 1 lb. (400 g) daikon – 1 lb. (400 g) purple cabbage – 1 tbsp (25 g) whole sea salt

Difficulty

Prep Time
10 minutes

Cooking Time
0 minutes

1. It is best to use a press to prepare the fermented vegetables, as it helps the liquid to come out of the vegetables; if you don't have one, anything heavy will do.

2. Scrub the carrots and the daikon, wash them separately from the cabbage and then dry them. Cut the root veg with a potato peeler and the cabbage with a sharp knife.

3. Put all the ingredients in the press, add salt, and press down. Leave them to stand in a warm place (about 68 degrees F/20 degrees C); wait until the vegetables are submerged in their liquids and for the lactic fermentation that gives the vegetables a sour and aromatic flavor to start. It usually takes 2-3 days, after which you can put the vegetables in a jar and keep in the fridge.

4. You can use them to pep up salads or eat a couple of forkfuls as an appetizer.

5. Fermented vegetables are one of the best foods to strengthen the bacterial flora and help normal intestinal fluid balance.

Stuffed Eggplant

Servings

4 eggplants - 1 1/2 cups (150 g) red rice - 1 oz. (30 g) pine nuts - 1 finely chopped onion - 2 oz. (50 g) oat cream - 2 1/2 tbsp (20 g) breadcrumbs - 4 tbsp (40 g) extra virgin olive oil - salt - pepper

Difficulty

Prep Time 10 minutes

Cooking Time about 60 minutes

1. Pre-heat the oven to 390 degrees F (200 degrees C). Wash the rice and boil for 30 minutes in hot water, then drain.

2. Wash the eggplants. Cut the bottom so that it stands up and the top just after the stalk. Scoop out the flesh to make a sort of container. Boil for 5 minutes and drain.

3. Finely chop the eggplant flesh; fry in a pan with the onion, oat cream and rice. Salt and pepper to taste.

4. Leave the flavors to absorb for 5 minutes, add the pine nuts and then stuff the eggplants with the mixture; top with breadcrumbs. Put in the oven for 20-30 minutes and serve.

Cream of Leek and Pumpkin
with a Sprinkling of Sautéed Scallions

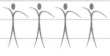

Servings

10 oz. (300 g) pumpkin flesh – 2 small leeks – 2 oz. (50 g) brown rice 1 scallion – 3 tbsp (30 g) pumpkin seeds – 2 tbsp (20 g) linseed oil – salt – pepper

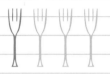

Difficulty

1. Cut the pumpkin into pieces, wash and cut the leeks into rounds. Put them into 2 pints of water together with the rice and cook covered over a low heat until the ingredients begin to flake. Add salt and pepper to taste.

2. The soup should be cooked gently and slowly. Stir regularly. After about 2 hours the soup will be thick and creamy: remove from the heat and add the oil.

3. Just before serving the soup, slice the scallion and sauté it in a non-stick pan; add the pumpkin seeds and after about 2 minutes season the soup with the mixture.

**Prep Time
10 minutes**

**Cooking Time
120 minutes**

Leek and Zucchini Salad Rolls with Orange

Servings

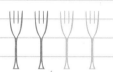

Difficulty

Prep Time
20 minutes

Cooking Time
20 minutes

1 organic orange – 1 large leek – 1 zucchini – 7 oz. (200 g) purple cabbage – 1 tbsp (10 g) sesame seeds – 2 tbsp (20 g) extra virgin olive oil

1. Wash the zucchini and the cabbage and cut into thin strips; do the same with half the orange rind and put to one side.

2. Wash and pull apart the leek to obtain leaves big enough to make the rolls (at least 2 per person). Remove the hard, green stringy part. Boil for 3 minutes in salted water to soften them.

3. Pre-heat the oven to 390 degrees F (200 degrees C). Pour the oil into a pan, add the vegetables and fry for 3-4 minutes. Remove from the heat and spread the mixture onto the leek leaves; roll them up and coat with the sesame seeds and orange rind.

4. Put the rolls into a baking tray lined with baking paper and put in the oven; cook for about 10 minutes and then serve with orange slices and any left-over vegetables.

Colorful Stir-fry Vegetables

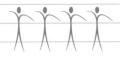

Servings

10 oz. (300 g) daikon – 1 carrot – 1 purple carrot – 7 oz. (200 g) cauliflower – 10 cherry tomatoes – 10 peanuts – 2 tbsp (20 g) extra virgin olive oil – salt – pepper

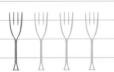

Difficulty

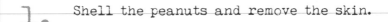

1. Shell the peanuts and remove the skin.

2. Trim, wash and carefully dry all the vegetables. Cut into pieces, rounds or sticks according to your own personal taste. Pour the oil into a non-stick pan and add the vegetables and peanuts.

3. Leave over a high heat for 5-7 minutes, mixing all the time so that they absorb the flavors and sauté lightly rather than burn. Add salt and pepper to taste and serve while still hot.

Prep Time
10 minutes

Cooking Time
5-7 minutes

Roast Vegetables with Soybean Cream

Servings

3.5 oz. (100 g) quinoa - 1 zucchini - half an eggplant - 2 boiled potatoes - 10 cherry tomatoes - 3.5 oz. (100 g) broccoli - 1 sprig of rosemary - 1 sprig of fresh oregano - 7 oz. (200 g) soy cream - 1 tbsp turmeric - 1 tsp mixed seeds: chia and linseeds - 2 tbsp (20 g) extra virgin olive oil - salt - chili pepper to taste

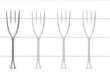

Difficulty

1. Trim the aromatic herbs and remove the hard, tough parts.

2. Boil the quinoa for 10 minutes, drain and pour into a bowl. Trim, wash and dry all the vegetables. Slice and cut as you like.

3. Dissolve the turmeric in the soy cream. Pre-heat the oven to 390 degrees F (200 degrees C) and grease a baking tray.

4. Mix all of the ingredients together, salt and add the seeds and freshly sliced chili pepper.

**Prep Time
10 minutes**

5. Pour the mixture into the baking tray, distribute evenly and cook in the oven for 20 minutes; remove from the oven and serve.

**Cooking Time
30 minutes**

With Fruit and Flours....

When there was still such a thing as a late morning or afternoon snack, we ate seasonal fruit, usually accompanied by a slice of bread: bread and grapes, bread with figs or plums and so on. Our grandmothers knew everything about nutrition; in fact, experts recommend eating fruit either before a meal or as a snack during the day. Each month nature offers us a variety of different fresh fruit and today, with globalization and large-scale retail stores, we can find our favorite fruit anywhere and at any time of the year. However, it is always better to eat local, seasonal fruits more often.

Fruits are indispensable in a vegan diet, they enrich it, and in addition to their natural goodness, they are the basis of many dishes, from desserts to juices, smoothies and purees. Even dried fruit (walnuts, almonds, pistachios, pine nuts and hazelnuts) are an outstanding resource to draw from for a balanced diet and an energetic and harmonious body.

Dried Apple and Cranberry Bars

Servings

2 apples – 2 oz. (50 g) fresh cranberries – 1 tbsp (about 15 g) dried cranberries

Difficulty

Prep Time
20 minutes

Cooking Time
60 minutes

1. Pre-heat the oven to 350 degrees F (180 degrees C) and line a baking tray with baking paper. Wash and peel the apples and cut them into small pieces.

2. Put the pieces of apple in the oven to dry, but don't let them darken in color; if necessary lower the temperature. Check on them regularly and after about an hour take them out of the oven.

3. In the meantime, trim, wash and dry the cranberries, then mash them with a fork. Add to the apples together with the dried cranberries and mix the ingredients well.

4. Spread out a sheet of plastic wrap on a smooth surface; spread the mixture on top and cover; transfer to a container of your choice. Leave to stand for about 3 hours with a weight on top.

5. Transfer the mixture to the fridge, still with the weight on top, and leave for at least a day before cutting it.

Stuffed Cookies

Servings

8 vegan millet puff cookies - 5 pitted dates - 1 oz. (30 g) almond flour - 1 oz. (30 g) chopped almonds - 1 tbsp (15 g) oat flakes - 1 tbsp (about 15 g) rum - 2 tbsp (20 g) grape juice

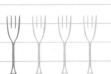

Difficulty

Prep Time
15 minutes

Cooking Time
0 minutes

1. Blend the dates, oats, rum and grape juice. Stir the almond flour into the mixture and put a generous amount of filling between each pair of cookies.

2. Pour the chopped almonds onto a plate and roll the cookies in them to cover the filling in the middle.

3. Put in the freezer for about an hour and you will have an ice cold dessert, perfect for a wicked snack.

4. If you want to make these cookies for the kids, substitute the rum with the same amount of grape juice or almond milk.

Mandarin and Chili Marmalade

Jars

3 lb. (1.5 kg) organic mandarins - 7 oz. (200 g) organic kumquats - 1 cup (200 g) cane sugar - 2 fresh medium - hot chili peppers (or add to taste)

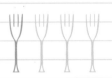

Difficulty

1. Wash the mandarins. Cut half of them in half and squeeze them, collect the juice and remove the seeds. Cut up the remaining fruit, leaving the rind. Wash the kumquats, slice them and remove the seeds.

Prep Time
10 minutes

2. Wash the chili peppers, remove the stalk and seeds and chop into small pieces. Put them in a pot together with the sugar; add all of the other ingredients and cook for about an hour. Stir regularly to ensure that the marmalade doesn't stick to the bottom.

3. When the peel of the citrus fruits becomes soft and the texture is to your liking, remove from heat and pour into the jars; put the lids on and sterilize the jars by boiling them for about 20 minutes.

Cooking Time
80 minutes

4. Leave to cool and store in a cool, dark place.

Banana and Date Custard with Fresh Fruit

Servings

10 dates – 1 banana – 1 peach – 2 apricots – 2 plums – 8 strawberries – 1 lemon

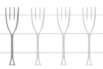

Difficulty

Prep Time
15 minutes

Cooking Time
0 minutes

1. Wash the apricots and remove the seeds, pit the dates, peel the banana and blend them all.

2. Divide the mixture into four portions and leave to cool in the freezer for about 2 hours.

3. Trim, wash and pat-dry all the other fruit with kitchen roll. Cut them into small pieces and put them in a bowl, covering them with lemon juice.

4. When you are ready to serve, prepare the desserts in portions. Arrange a layer of fruit first and then add a layer of date custard, followed by another layer of fruit. The dessert can either be served ice cold or after having been left to soften.

Walnut Stuffed Figs

Servings

12 hard, ripe figs - 12 walnut kernels - 2 kiwis - 4 medium-hot chili peppers - 3 tbsp (45 g) malt or maple syrup

Difficulty

1. Wash the chili peppers and cut them into rounds. Wash the figs and make a cross-cut at the top. Insert a walnut kernel and one or two slices of chili pepper into each one.

2. Put the figs into an ovenproof dish.

3. You can eat them as they are or sweeten them, at room temperature or baked in the oven for 10 minutes at 430 degrees F (220 degrees C). Wash and slice the kiwis; use them as a base to serve the figs on.

4. Stuffed figs are delicious either hot or at room temperature, and they are really easy to make!

Prep Time
5 minutes

Cooking Time
(if desired)
10 minutes

Mock Carob Bean Chocolates

Servings

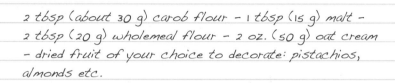

2 tbsp (about 30 g) carob flour - 1 tbsp (15 g) malt -
2 tbsp (20 g) wholemeal flour - 2 oz. (50 g) oat cream
- dried fruit of your choice to decorate: pistachios,
almonds etc.

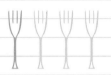

Difficulty

1. Sieve the carob flour into a saucepan. Add the malt, wholemeal flour and oat cream.

2. Stir until the mixture is smooth, soft and lump-free. Bring to the boil, stirring continuously, and remove from the heat immediately.

3. Pour into molds of your choice, decorate with the dried fruit and put in the fridge to set.

4. When the mock chocolates are set you can either turn them out or leave them in the molds, and then serve.

Prep Time
10 minutes

Cooking Time
3-5 minutes

Drunken and Dry Fruit

Servings

4 peaches – 4 plums – 8 strawberries – 7 fl oz. (2 dl)
white wine – 2 lemons – 2 apricots – 1 apple

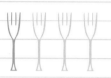

Difficulty

**Prep Time
10 minutes**

**Cooking Time
20 minutes**

1. Pre-heat the oven to 480 degrees F (250 degrees C). Line a baking tray with wax paper. Wash and dry the apple and apricots, cut into slices, spread out on the tray and put in the oven.

2. Turn the apples after about 5 minutes and the apricots after 10 minutes. Take the apples out of the oven after about another 5 minutes and the apricots after 10 minutes. Leave to cool.

3. Wash, dry and cut the rest of the fruit into small pieces, put into a bowl and pour in the wine and freshly squeezed lemon juice.

4. Divide between the glasses and serve at room temperature, together with the dried fruit.

Poached Pears in Spiced White Wine

Servings

2 large or 3 medium pears – 1 organic orange – 5 cloves –
1 cinnamon stick (about 2 cm) – 1 tbsp (15 g) cane sugar –
1 pt. (5 dl) sweet white wine (Moscato)

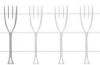

Difficulty

**Prep Time
10 minutes**

**Cooking Time
20-30
minutes**

1. Wash the pears and the orange. Cut the pear into pieces. Cut the orange rind into enough matchsticks to fill a tablespoon.

2. Squeeze the citrus fruit and filter the juice into a pot.

3. Add the spices, pears, wine, rind and sugar; cook over a low heat until the pears reach the desired consistency (20 to 30 minutes is usually long enough).

4. Remove from the heat, leave to cool down a bit and then serve.

Strawberry and Banana Strudel

Servings

10 oz. (300 g) vegan puff pastry - 2 bananas - 7 oz. (200 g) strawberries - 4 tbsp (40 g) chopped hazelnuts - 4 pitted dates

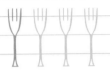

Difficulty

Prep Time
15 minutes

Cooking Time
25 minutes

1. Trim, wash and pat-dry the strawberries with kitchen roll and cut into pieces. Peel the bananas and cut into rounds.

2. Pre-heat the oven to 390 degrees F (200 degrees C). Line a baking tray with baking paper. Unroll the puff pastry and lay it out on a suitable work surface.

3. Blend the dates and put the mixture into the center of the pastry. Put the fruit and half of the chopped hazelnuts on top of it. Fold the pastry in a way that the juices don't leak during cooking. Sprinkle the remaining chopped hazelnuts on the top.

4. Put in the oven and cook for about 25 minutes. Remove from the oven and leave to cool before slicing.

Oat Cake with Goji Berries and Lemon

Servings

2 oz. (50 g) oat flakes – 1 oz. (30 g) coconut flour – 1 oz. (30 g) almond flour – 2 oz. (50 g) wholemeal flour – 3.5 fl oz. (1 dl) coconut or almond milk – 5 tbsp (50 g) corn oil – 2 tbsp (20 g) Goji berries – rind of 1 lemon – 1.5 tsp (5 g) yeast for cakes

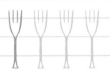

Difficulty

1. Pre-heat the oven to 350 degrees F (180 degrees C) and line a cake tin with baking paper. Soak the Goji berries in the milk for about 5 minutes.

2. Mix the flours and the oil in a bowl. Drain the berries and add the milk to the mixture together with the oat flakes. Mix the ingredients well. Finally, add the yeast, the berries and the lemon rind.

Prep Time
15 minutes

3. Pour the mixture into the cake tin and put into the oven. Bake for about 30 minutes and then remove from the oven; leave to stand for 5 minutes and transfer the cake onto a cake plate. Wait until it has cooled down completely before cutting.

Cooking Time
30 minutes

Pistachio and Almond Cakes

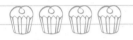

Cakes

2 oz. (50 g) wholemeal flour – 2 oz. (50 g) almond flour – 2 oz. (50 g) coconut flour – 80 g (50 + 30) chopped pistachios – 3.5 fl oz. (1 dl) coconut or almond milk – 1 oz. (30 g) sliced almonds –2 tsp (6 g) yeast for cakes – 1 tbsp (10 g) extra virgin olive oil

Difficulty

Prep Time
20 minutes

Cooking Time
30 minutes

1. Divide the wholemeal flour, the coconut flour and the almond milk equally between two bowls. Pre-heat the oven to 350 degrees F (180 degrees C).

2. Take a 4-portion mold or 4 single-portion ovenproof dishes and grease them with a drop of oil. Cover the bottom and sides of two of them with the chopped pistachios (1 oz./30 g), and the other two with the sliced almonds.

3. Mix the mixtures in the two bowls really well: to one add the almond flour and to the other the left-over chopped pistachios. Add the yeast and divide the mixtures equally among the molds or dishes.

4. Bake for 30 minutes and then take out of the oven; leave them to cool down before turning out.

Dark Chocolate and Coconut Cakes

Cakes

3.5 oz. (100 g) oat flour - 2 oz. (50 g) coconut flour - 2 oz. (50 g) oat cream - 2 tbsp (about 30 g) malt - 1.5 tsp (5 g) yeast for cakes - 2 oz. (50 g) dark chocolate - optional: 2 fl oz. (0.5 dl) coconut milk or oat milk or cognac

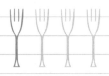

Difficulty

Prep Time
10 minutes

Cooking Time
25 minutes

1. Break the chocolate into four pieces. Pre-heat the oven to 350 degrees F (180 degrees C).

2. Pour the oat flour into a bowl, add 2/3 of the coconut flour and stir in the malt, oat cream and yeast.

3. Mix well until the mixture is smooth and lump-free. If it is too dry, soften it with two or three tablespoons of coconut or oat milk, or if you prefer a more aromatic flavor you can use a spirit such as cognac.

4. Grease the bottom and sides of a 4-portion mold (or 4 single molds) and cover with the remaining coconut flour. Fill half of each mold with the cream, add a piece of chocolate to each and put in the oven.

5. Leave to cook for about 25 minutes and then take out of the oven; leave to cool down for about 5 minutes before turning out.

Almond and Hazelnut Cakes with Peaches

Cakes

2 oz. (50 g) buckwheat flour - 2 oz. (50 g) oat flour - 2 oz. (50 g) hazelnut flour - 3.5 fl oz. (1 dl) almond milk - 2 tbsp (20 g) chopped hazelnuts - 2 peaches - 4 tbsp (20 g) cane sugar - 1.5 tsp (5 g) yeast for cakes

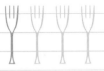

Difficulty

Prep Time
10 minutes

Cooking Time
20-25
minutes

1. Wash the peaches and cut them into slices. Pre-heat the oven to 350 degrees F (180 degrees C).

2. Mix the buckwheat, oat and hazelnut flours in a bowl. When they are evenly mixed, slowly add the almond milk and stir until the mixture is smooth and lump-free; add the yeast.

3. Line 4 single-portion dishes with baking paper, half fill with the mixture and decorate with the peach slices, chopped hazelnuts and sugar.

4. Put in the oven and bake for about 20-25 minutes, checking every now and then that the cakes aren't drying out or burning.

5. Remove from the oven and leave to cool before turning out.

Oat Cakes with Raspberries and Cranberry

Cakes

2 oz. (60 g) oat flakes – 1 oz. (30 g) millet flour –
2 tbsp malt (about 30 g) – 3.5 fl oz. (1 dl) oat milk –
1 tbsp cranberries (about 15 g) – 3.5 oz. (100 g) raspberries –
1 oz. (30 g) soya butter – 1.5 tsp (5 g) yeast for cakes –
1 tbsp (10 g) extra virgin olive oil

Difficulty

1. Pre-heat the oven to 350 degrees F (180 degrees C) and grease 4 single-portion dishes. Dissolve the yeast in warm milk.

2. Mix the oat flakes with the millet flour and wet with the milk; add the malt and room-temperature butter. When the mixture is well mixed, add the cranberries and half of the raspberries.

3. Divide the mixture between the dishes and sprinkle with the remaining raspberries.

4. Bake for 20-25 minutes; take out of the oven and leave to cool before turning out.

Prep Time
10 minutes

Cooking Time
20-25
minutes

The Author

A naturopath, freelance journalist and photographer specializing in wine and food itineraries, CINZIA TRENCHI has collaborated in the writing of numerous recipe books published by Italian and foreign publishing houses. A passionate cook, she has also worked for many Italian magazines covering regional, traditional, macrobiotic and natural cuisine specialties, providing both the text and the photographs, and including dishes of her own creation. Her recipe books include original and creative meals. They propose new flavor associations and unusual pairings that result in unique preparations that keep with the spirit of flavor without forgetting the nutritional properties of foods, in order to achieve the best equilibrium during a meal and the consequent improvement in well-being. She lives in Monferrato, in the Piedmont region, in a home immersed in greenery. Using the flowers, aromatic herbs and vegetables grown in her garden, she prepares original sauces and condiments, in addition to decorations for her dishes, allowing herself to be guided by the seasons and her knowledge of the earth's fruits. With White Star Publishers she has published "Gluten-Free, Gourmet Recipes"; "Fat-Free, Gourmet Recipes"; "Chili Pepper, Moments of Spicy Passion"; "My Favorite Recipes"; "Smoothies & Juices, Health and Energy in a Glass"; "Hamburgers, 50 Easy Recipes"; "Mug Cakes, Sweet & Savory Recipes"; "Detox, Practical Tips and Recipes for Clean Eating"; and Superfoods, Healthy, Nourishing and Energizing Recipes".

Index of Ingredients

WHITE STAR PUBLISHERS

WS White Star Publishers® is a registered trademark
Property of De Agostini Libri S.p.A.

© 2016 De Agostini Libri S.p.A.
Via G. da Verrazano, 15
28100 Novara, Italy
www.whitestar.it – www.deagostini.it

Translation and Editing: TperTradurre s.r.l.

ISBN 978-88-544-1070-1
1 2 3 4 5 6   20 19 18 17 16

Printed in China

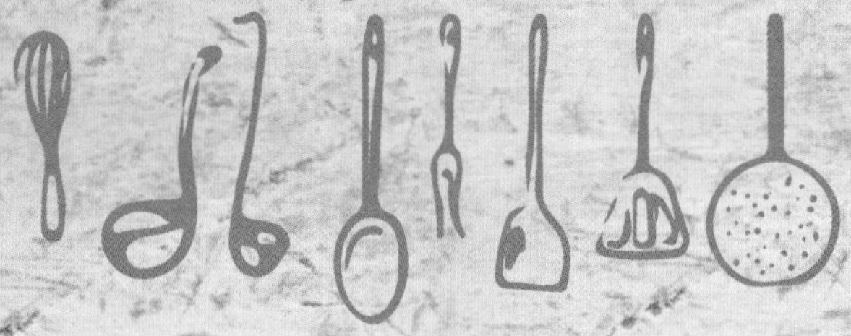